MEDIÆVAL
COLCHESTER'S
LOST LANDMARKS

MEDIÆVAL
COLCHESTER'S
LOST LANDMARKS

John Ashdown-Hill

For my mother, and in memory of my father,
who between them encouraged me to look for
the signs of the past.

First published in Great Britain in 2009 by The Breedon Books Publishing Company Limited
Breedon House, 3 The Parker Centre, Derby, DE21 4SZ.

This paperback edition published in Great Britain in 2014 by DB Publishing,
an imprint of JMD Media Ltd

A catalogue record for this book is available from the British Library.

ISBN 978-1-78091-402-2

Printed and bound in Great Britain by Marston Book Services Ltd, Oxfordshire

CONTENTS

ILLUSTRATIONS

Unless otherwise credited, photographs and drawings are by the author and engravings and artifacts are from the author's collection.

57. The 14th-century nave of St Nicholas's Church (© Colchester and Ipswich Museums).

58. The central tower of the mediaeval St Nicholas's Church in 1669.

59. 'James', the 15th-century *sanctus* bell from St Nicholas's Church.

60. 'John', the great 15th-century bell from St Nicholas's Church.

61. The bellfounder's mark of the Hilles on 'John'.

62. A stone from St Nicholas's Church.

63. The 19th-century north tower of St Nicholas's Church.

64. Whitefriars Cross, Hereford.

65. The site of the stone cross in the churchyard of St Peter's.

66. Newark Cross.

67. Plaque in Frere Street (the High Street).

68. A mediaeval bastion in More Street (Priory Street).

69. Colchester Castle in the mid-17th century.

70. Colchester Castle today.

71. Plaque marking the site of Head Gate.

72. The site of Head Gate.

73. The site of East Gate.

74. Plaque marking the site of East Gate.

75. Schere Gate in the early 20th century.

76. The postern gate in More Street (Priory Street).

77. The Moot Hall.

78. A Colchester watermill in use for fulling, 1777.

79. Middle Mill in the early 20th century.

80. The abbot of Glastonbury's fish house at Meare in Somerset (engraving from P. Ward, *Somerset*, London 1928).

81. A Colchester watermill, 1767.

82. The Hythe in the early 20th century.

83. 'Timperleys'.

84. Part of a mediaeval shopfront.

85. Former almshouses in Eld Lane.

86. 'The Craftsman' and the east side of Trinity Street.

87. 'Timbers' Restaurant.

88. The sign of the Bull Inn.

89. The back courtyard of the Bull Inn.

90. A mediaeval classroom (woodcut from John Holt's *Lac Puerorum*, *c*.1495, courtesy of Geoffrey Wheeler).
91. A performing bear.
92. Dogs attacking a bear.
93. A mediaeval stews (redrawn from a mediaeval woodcut by Geoffrey Wheeler).
94. Male head (Holy Trinity Church).
95. Female head (Holy Trinity Church).
96. Mediaeval-style playing cards.
97. Pectoral Cross of Abbot Beche, last abbot of Colchester. (Image courtesy of the abbot and Benedictine community of Buckfast Abbey, Devon).
98. After vespers: a modern congregation in St John's Abbey Gatehouse.
99. Mediaeval money (pennies, half-groat, groat and angel).
100. Stones from St John's Abbey.

LIST OF ABBREVIATIONS

BL	The British Library
B. *OB*	Benham, ed., *The Oath Book or Red Parchment Book of Colchester*
ERO	Essex Record Office
HHB	Crawford, ed., *The Household Books of John Howard*
L & P	*Letters & Papers Foreign & Domestic*
OB	*The Oath Book or Red Parchment Book of Colchester* (original MS)
RCHM	*Royal Commission for Historical Monuments*
Soc. Ant.	The Society of Antiquaries of London
TNA	The National Archives
VCH	The Victoria County History

ACKNOWLEDGEMENTS

I owe a large debt of gratitude to previous researchers into Colchester's history, particularly Philip Morant in the 18th century and William Gurney Benham in the early 20th century. I am also indebted to the writers of the *Victoria County History of Essex*, vols 2 (Religious Houses) and 9 (Colchester), to Dr Chris Thornton (editor of the *Victoria County History of Essex* and supervisor of my PhD thesis) and to Jane Bedford of the Essex Record Office. I would also like to thank those who have kindly helped me with illustrations: Colchester Archaeological Trust, Colchester and Ipswich Museums, John Carter, Peter Froste and Geoffrey Wheeler, together with Cath D'Alton who produced the published versions of my plans. My thanks are also due to Annette Carson, Bernard Cuthbert and Dave Perry who have helped me by visiting sites, taking measurements and reading and correcting various drafts of the text.

INTRODUCTION

Colchester has a long history – the longest recorded history of any town in Britain – and it is justly proud of its importance in the Roman era. However, the strong modern emphasis on Colchester's Roman heritage has sometimes been at the expense of other periods as popular histories of the town often focus heavily on the Romans. They may perhaps go on to include a brief mention of the building of the castle and of two religious houses that lay outside the town walls in the Norman period. After that, the next landmark in many published accounts is the siege of Colchester during the English Civil War. The unsuspecting reader is suddenly catapulted forward into the 17th century across an astonishing time gap of more than 500 years. It is as though mediaeval Colchester had no history worth reporting, which is simply not true. The surviving town records offer an incomparable picture of Colchester in the mediaeval period, and the only reason why so many writers have neglected this seems to be that reading these records – in difficult handwriting and in Latin – requires a certain amount of effort.

At the same time town planners, archaeologists and the authorities of the Anglican Church seem to have conspired to obscure the town's mediaeval past by obliterating its visible traces. Scant thought has been spared for Colchester's mediaeval edifices when they were still standing, while their ruins and foundations were often quickly shunted aside in a quest for financial gain or for what were perceived as the more important Roman remains beneath. As recently as the 1950s, in an appalling act of wanton destruction, an important and historic town centre church was demolished. Although this building had certainly been restored and enlarged by the Victorians, we shall see in due course that a significant proportion of its structure at the time of its demolition still dated from the 14th century. It was a church in which John Howard, Duke of Norfolk (*c*.1422–1485), the friend and ally of Richard III, used to worship. On both historical and architectural grounds it certainly should have been preserved and its loss, coming on top of the much earlier destruction of the town's greatest religious buildings (the abbey and the two great priories of St Botolph and Greyfriars), was a catastrophe for Colchester's visible mediaeval heritage. Many other buildings from the mediaeval period have likewise entirely disappeared, with the result that a significant portion of the town's history is currently lost to view.

This book attempts to redress the balance by recapturing in print and images the vanished appearance of mediaeval Colchester, thus putting back into place an important slice of the town's history. I have tried to make my picture of late mediaeval Colchester as complete as possible so the book is not just about lost churches, important though these may have been. Alongside abbeys and priories we shall also rediscover inns and brothels, dwellings and dunghills. Curiously, the process of rediscovery shows that some of the sights of the mediaeval town which one might actually have thought and hoped were now a thing of the past have in fact returned to haunt the town centre in an updated guise. We shall learn that the contents of Robert Cok's mediaeval *pissepotts* and the offal, which the town butchers discarded in the castle ditch, do have their modern equivalents in 21st-century Colchester.

My own historical interest focuses chiefly on the 15th century. For that reason, and because the term 'Middle Ages' covers quite a long period (and can indeed be somewhat elastic) I have chosen to concentrate principally on evoking the appearance of Colchester's lost features as they would have been towards the end of the 15th century. This has two possible advantages. Firstly the date corresponds roughly with what has generally been perceived as the end of the Middle Ages in England and secondly it allows us to look at the magnificent religious buildings of Colchester at their apogee, before they were wrecked by the greed and vandalism of Henry VIII. However, the picture I shall present is not exclusively 15th century, and where possible I will also trace interesting developments during the earlier Middle Ages.

In fact, thanks to the inestimable and almost untapped resource represented by the surviving court rolls of mediaeval Colchester, a great deal more could probably be said about the earlier period. Despite the recent regrettable removal of this resource from Colchester to Chelmsford, I for one would be delighted if my present foray into the lost world of mediaeval Colchester were to encourage other researchers to delve further and to discover earlier material that I have missed. Who knows whether such new work might not yet uncover the mysterious appearance and function of the vanished *whirlegigges* or reveal the location of the tennis court of mediaeval Colchester.

It is my hope that this book will be accessible to everyone, and with that in mind I have also tried to build into the text explanations of specialised vocabulary. In an attempt to avoid overloading the book with footnotes, material which has been previously published in the VCH is usually referenced only to that publication (which in turn will supply details of the original source). However, material from other published sources, together with previously unpublished 'new' information, has been fully referenced so that those with a scholarly interest can consult my sources if they wish. Where possible, mediaeval Colchester court rolls references have been cross-referenced to W. Gurney Benham's unpublished, translated 'transcripts' of these rolls (also kept at the Essex Record Office). While these 'transcripts' have some omissions, they are probably more accessible for most readers than the mediaeval Latin of the original rolls. In the case of the court roll for 1446–47, however, Benham's 'transcript' is too abbreviated to be useful.

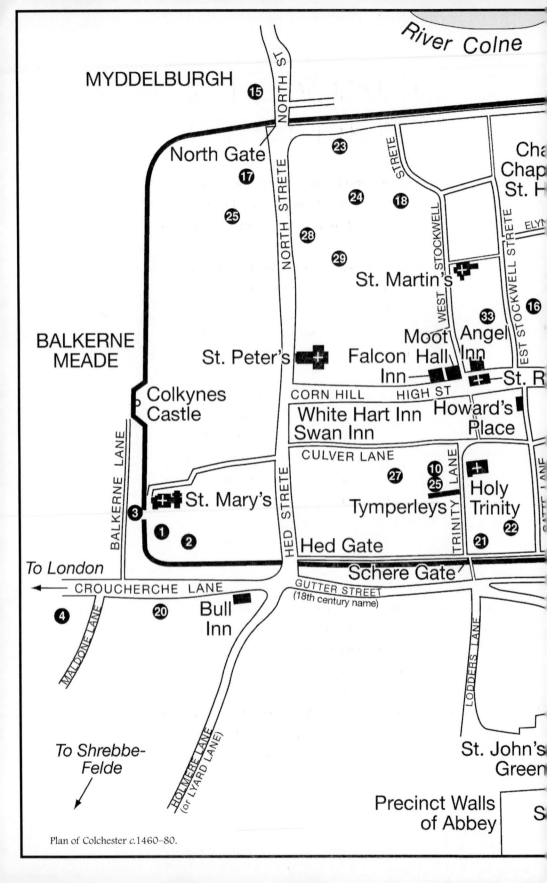

Plan of Colchester c.1460–80.

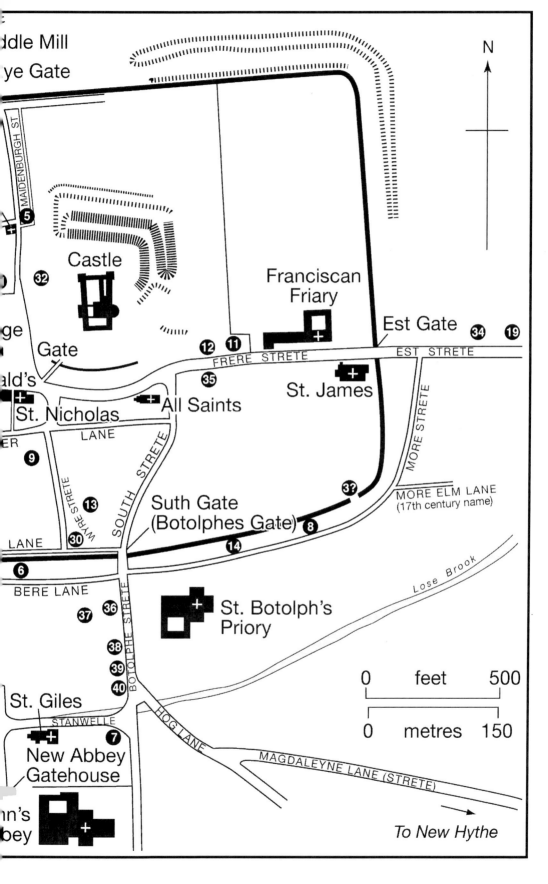

Plan of Colchester *c.*1460~80 – Key

(Some locations within streets are approximate.)

1   School in this area.

2   St Andrew's Chapel in this area.

3   Postern Gate in this area.

4   Church (later Priory) of the Holy Cross (Guild of St Helen).

5   House of Roger Purtepet (Purpyt), town clerk, 1463–81.

6   Tenements of John Tanner and Matilda Doraunt (*née* Sayher) and garden of Richard Lyard, 1463/64.

7   Barbican.

8   *Rentaria* and gardens of Richard Barber, 1466/67.

9   Houses and barn of Roger Purpyt (as tenant of John Seman), John Boteler, Matthew Drury, Thomas Hervey, Roger London, John Horn, John Levyngton, Robert Porter, William Gossefeld, Peter William, Robert Sayer, John Skelton, John Bryan and John Nicoll, Culver Lane, 1466/67.

10 House of John Parker (or Parkes) opposite Holy Trinity Church (prior to 1481).

11 Tenement of Raphael and Johanna Vanell (formerly of John Pake), 1466/67.

12 Two shops, 1466/67.

13 Tenement of William Bonefaunt senior and Margery Bonefaunt, 1465.

14 Six *renteres* of William Bonefaunt senior, 1465.

15 Three tenements, one each belonging to William and Eleanor Gamday, Robert Payne and John Abell. Moorland of John Sayer behind (to the west), 1480/81.

16 Three tenements, one belonging to John Roper senior and two to Thomas and Margaret Baroun, East Stockwell Street. Garden of John Stevene behind (to the east), 1480.

17 Tenement and garden of Thomas and Lucy Profite (1480), later of Thomas and Margaret Wolferton, then of John and Ellen Thusk, 1481.

18 Messuage of Thomas Shaket, two rentars of Walter and Joan Lopham and footpath of Richard Markes, W. Stockwell Street, 1481.

19 Two messuages of Ellen Hubert (*née* Chercheman) and John Cherecheman junior, messuage of William Hunt of Ardeley, messuage of Roger Pekam and 'Bentfeld' belonging to John Drewe, 1481.

20 Tenement and garden, rentar and garden of Thomas and Agnes Balstone and rentar of John Dowe, 1467.

21 Tenement of John Hervy, tenement of John and Joan Ody (with access to Eldelane *via le Burgate*) and rentar of John Ody, 1480. [Burgate tenement granted to William & Alice Prentice, then to William & Alice Reignold, 1481].

22 Gardens of Richard Whithermerssh with almshouses to the east, 1481.

23 Tenement of John Joyce; rentar, tenement, curtilege and garden of John and Margaret Boseveld and tenement of Thomas Wolferton, gent., 1481.

24 'Moor' or garden of Richard Markes, 1480–81.

25 Land belonging to Joseph Elianore's Chantry, 1481.

26 Rectory of Holy Trinity Church, 1481.

27 Garden of Margery Sparwe, 1481.

28 Two tenements of John and Elizabeth Litewyn, 1483.

29 Grange and garden belonging to Joseph Elianore's Chantry and land of St Helen's Guild, 1483.

30 Land of Nicholas Clere and tenement of John Payne, Wyre Street, 1483.

31 Rentar of William Dowall, messuage of Richard and Matilda Maidstone and tenement of John Baker with access to market place, 1479.

32 Rentar of John Baker, tenement of Richard Dykman and rentar of Richard and Matilda Maidstone, all backing onto land of Colchester Castle, 1479.

33 Tenements of William Jamys and John Aldham and two tenements of Robert and Agnes Cokke, with land of Richard Ball behind (to the west), 1485.

34 Tenements of Robert and Rose Baker, of William Flyngaunt and of Agnes Polewik, with land belonging to Colchester Castle behind (to the north).

35 John and Robert Shipman, 1481.

36 The Bear Stake, Bear Hall and Bear Garden.

37 Licensed Colchester brothels.

38 Tenement of John Carter, smith, and later (1473) of Nicholas Sayer, draper.

39 Tenement, rentar and garden of John and Margaret Vykery (1473) and later of Thomas and Alice Hobelot (1474).

40 Tenement of Thomas Gameney and later (1473) of Thomas Hobelot, weaver.

'PLEASANTLY LOCATED AND WELL-WATERED'

It may be useful to begin with one or two observations about the town name of *Colchester*. The modern name is of Latin origin. However, it is only indirectly derived from the Roman name for the town and came into being in the early mediaeval period.

It is often stated that the Roman name for Colchester was *Camulodunum*. This is not strictly correct. The name *Camulodunum* is not a Roman (Latin) word, but comes from the Ancient British language. It was the pre-Roman name of the fortified town of the Trinovantes in the vicinity of modern Lexden. Initially the Roman settlement was named *Colonia Claudia* in honour of the Emperor Claudius, who conquered Britain. Later the town was renamed *Colonia Victricensis* to celebrate its recapture from the forces of Queen Boudicca.

The modern name of *Colchester* is derived not from the Ancient British *Camulodunum*, but, like Cologne in Germany, is a corruption of the Latin word for this particular type of town, *Colonia*. In the case of Colchester the *Colon-* element eventually became combined with another Latin word *castra*, meaning camp.

Colchester was the first capital of the Roman province of Britain, and although it soon lost this pre-eminence, in the early Middle Ages it was certainly the chief town of Essex. The Domesday map of Essex accords pride of place to Colchester, at a time when Chelmsford did not exist. Not until the 13th century did the latter become recognised as the county town.

Colchester stands on the banks of the River Colne, 'at the upper limit of navigation and the lowest crossing point'.[1] The low-lying lands adjacent to the river are water meadows, rightly regarded as unsuitable for building upon. Sadly, in recent years this land has begun to be exploited for housing developments. If the unfortunate residents of the newly erected dwellings have not yet become aware that they are living in the flood plain it is probably only a matter of time before this fact becomes unpleasantly apparent to them. Even in the Middle Ages the land near the river used to flood and just a little ill-advised human intervention could be sufficient to cause problems. Thus, it is recorded that the dam at Middle Mill caused the neighbouring fields to be flooded in 1473/4.[2]

Victorian drinking fountain, East Hill.

Colchester's watery associations were well-recognised in the past. In the reign of King William II (1087–1100) a charter relating to the foundation of St John's Abbey[3] conjures a delightful picture of Colchester's then still sylvan setting, describing the town as 'situated in the eastern region of Britain; a town near a port; pleasantly located, well-watered with gushing springs all around; with most healthy air, built with the strongest town walls'.[4] By the later Middle Ages the water from the Colne itself, though plentiful and close at hand, was not safe for drinking because offal and other waste products were disposed of in the river. This practice was banned, but the fact that there were fairly frequent prosecutions proves that it remained a health hazard. In 1463–64, for example, William Baker was fined for throwing dung into the river at the Hythe.[5] However, although the river water was unsuitable to be drunk 'raw', water from the Colne was certainly used in the brewing of beer and for other domestic purposes.

Some properties in Colchester, including a few lucky private dwellings, either enjoyed exclusive possession of their own water sources or shared a well with one or two other houses. Thus, in 1481 John Boseveld and his wife Margaret (*née* Cely) owned both a freehold property and a second house which was let to a tenant in the parish of St Peter. These two houses were adjoined by their own garden, which was enclosed by a wall and the dwellings had half rights in a shared well.[6] Both the castle and the Franciscan priory were also in the enviable position of owning their own private water sources.

However, the majority of households had recourse to communal sources of water only. There were at least four public wells within easy reach of the town centre in the Middle Ages: St Helen's Well (in St Helen's Lane), All Saints' Well near All Saints' Church, the Stock Well (which gave its name to East and West Stockwell Streets) and a well in Trinity Lane. There may also have been others. A little to the west of the Church of St James the Great, opposite the Greyfriars site, the remains of a Victorian drinking fountain can still be seen today built into the wall beside the road. This may mark the site of a water source which was in use in the Middle Ages.

There were also wells outside the town walls. Adjacent to Magdalen Street (the main road leading from Colchester to its port at the New Hythe) was Child Well.[7] Beyond the town wall on the southern side there were two wells: Berstake Well in *Bere Lane* (modern Vinyard Street) was close to the Bear Stake and the brothels.[8] A little further south towards St John's Abbey, the Stan Well was located 'in the highway opposite the abbot of St John's new tower'[9]: presumably in Stanwell Street (as it ran before Southway was constructed in the 1970s) and opposite the newly erected early 15th-century Abbey Gatehouse. To the west, not far from the postern gate in the town wall beside the Church of Our Lady-at-the-Wall,[10] was Balkerne Well while beyond East Gate there were no fewer than three wells. A large one was

Holy Well plaque at No. 39 Harwich Road.

located just outside the gate itself. There was also Duddeles Well in East Street, while further out from the town, on the road leading towards Harwich, Holy Well was to be found beside St Anne's Chapel. The site of this last well is still marked today by a plaque on the front of the house at No. 39 Harwich Road which reads 'HOLY WELL REOPENED 1844', though no sign of the well itself is now visible (from the road at least).

A public water course existed in Crouch Street (*Croucherchestret*) as the court rolls record a complaint in 1470–71 that it had been blocked.[11] This is probably the same water that is described, two years later, as flowing outside Head Gate in the direction of Maldon Lane with a well positioned there known as *Houndepet*.[12] The origin of the latter name may have been 'Hound Pit', or possibly 'Hound Put' from the Latin word *puteum* meaning 'well'. Water also flowed inside the town walls: down *Hedgatestrete* (modern Head Street), for example, in the direction of the town gate – though in 1473/4 there were two complaints that this flow had been diverted into Culver Lane (modern Culver Street West).[13] There was an aqueduct at the Hythe[14] and, in addition to the River Colne itself, there were also brooks in the suburbs outside the town walls.

One of these was called Lose Brook. Its name is revealed in a property transfer dated 22 November 1473 and, relating to dwelling houses with an enclosed garden, sited on the western side of St Botolph's Street.[15] The properties are described as adjacent to Lose Brook, which ran in a north-easterly direction in the little valley between St John's Abbey and the town wall, now in the vicinity of the present Southway as it nears the St Botolph's roundabout. It was perhaps Lose Brook (or a part of its water) which was the subject of a prosecution in 1463/4 when a watercourse was illicitly diverted to flow down *Magdaleyn Lane* (modern Magdalen Street).[16] Eighteenth-century maps indicate that Lose Brook rose (presumably from a spring) to the east of the Stan Well. It flowed through the precincts of St Botolph's Priory where some of its waters may well have been channelled through the priory's residential buildings for domestic purposes. Eventually it met the northern end of Brook Street (which was originally so named because of this). By the 18th century Lose Brook seems to have been channelled to pass beneath East Street in the approximate vicinity of the present mini-roundabout. At earlier periods there may perhaps have been a ford at this point. Lose Brook seems to have emptied itself into the River Colne by the mill pond at East Mill. Mediaeval records also contain mention of another brook called Slaggesbrook but where this ran is unclear.[17]

Beyond the suburbs there were streams in the countryside, and on some of these there were watermills (see chapter 6). The town's four administrative areas, or wards,[18] were not confined to the area within the walls but stretched out into the suburbs and countryside beyond. In the rural part of the south ward there was a stream called *Brownesford rever*. In the 1470s this flowed through land held by William Heynes who was prosecuted for failing to maintain the riverbanks and for allowing them to become overgrown with rushes and trees.[19]

In addition to wells and brooks there were many ditches. These were supposed to be 'scoured' regularly, but their frequent mention in the mediaeval court rolls arises precisely from the fact that this scouring had often been neglected. For example, in 1476–78 there were complaints about unscoured ditches in *Shepynlane* (modern Sheepen Road),[20] while the Master and Guild of St Helen, who then had charge of the Hospital and Church of the Holy Cross in Crouch Street, were prosecuted for failing to scour the ditch by the wayside cross in *Maldon Lane* (modern Maldon Road).[21] Even the abbot of St John's and the prior of St Botolph's were called to account for unscoured ditches.

The ground around Colchester was, and still is, undulating. The walled town itself stood on elevated land. Outside the walls the ground fell away in all directions. However, there was rising ground to the west where the pre-Roman British settlement of *Camulodunum* had once stood. Likewise the ground first fell, then rose again quite rapidly to the south of Colchester's town wall in the direction of St John's Abbey. It also rose again in an easterly direction along the road leading towards Harwich. The royal forest of King's Wood grew on rising ground to the north of the town (where it was transected by the road leading towards Ipswich). Even in the vicinity of the New Hythe there was rising ground. For reasons which we can only imagine this was popularly known in the 15th century as 'Love Hill'.[22]

One aspect of Colchester's pleasant location was the existence within the town walls of open spaces with trees and plants. Even today Colchester enjoys the possession of a good deal of open space, though this is now increasingly under threat from the encroachment of builders and developers. However, much of the water meadow land south of Cowdray Avenue and north of the river remains untouched for the present, and even within the town walls there are still a number of large privately and publicly owned gardens.

The Colchester town walls enclose a relatively small area of just over 108 acres. Even so, by no means was all the space within the town walls occupied by buildings in the Middle Ages. In that period there were very extensive areas of open land and a number of large gardens and orchards producing fruit and vegetables. The north eastern quarter of the town had a great deal of green land, comprising the castle field (modern Castle Park) and the very extensive precinct, kitchen gardens and orchards of the Franciscan Priory (now lying beneath the houses and gardens of Roman Road and Castle Road). South of this, in the angle made by the eastern and southern walls of the town, was Berry Field. Towards the western end of the town there was a good deal of open ground in the vicinity of the Church of Our Lady-at-the-Wall. The churchyard itself contributed to this open space, as indeed did Colchester's other churchyards. Also the town's more substantial private houses, such as 'Tymperley's' and the Howard family residence (now the 'Red Lion') had gardens and orchards. Indeed, agricultural activities were carried on within the town walls and some farm buildings were interspersed among the houses. For example there was a barn called *Sperewygesberne* by St Helen's Well. Other barns were located in Holy Trinity parish and on North Hill next to St Peter's churchyard.

The greenery was as much a recognised feature of the landscape of mediaeval Colchester as the town's buildings. The fact that the land around the town was extensively wooded did not escape the notice of the king. To the north of the walled town stretched the forest of King's Wood, a large royal hunting preserve, small portions of which still survive (known nowadays as 'High Woods'). Modern Shrub

End derives its name from the fact that in the Middle Ages it was the site of a wood called *le Shrebbe*.[23] There were even trees growing quite close to the town walls by the 15th century – though at earlier periods, when the walls were still seen as the town's main defences, this would hardly have been allowed.

One of Colchester's notable late mediaeval landmarks was a great elm tree which grew just outside the town walls in More Street (modern Priory Street) near the junction with More Elm Lane.[24] More Street itself probably took its name from a nearby *more*. In mediaeval English this word can have the same meaning as its modern descendant 'moor', namely a piece of land that is waterlogged. However, it also had a more general meaning covering any stretch of land than was left uncultivated. A number of *mores* are mentioned in the surviving records of mediaeval Colchester. There was one in what is now the Lower Castle Park in the vicinity of the boating lake where the land probably was waterlogged (as it sometimes still is today). Another *more* was located somewhere within the parish of St Nicholas.[25] This one seems not to have been waterlogged, for it eventually became a garden (while yet retaining its old name of *Le More*). The More Street *more* was perhaps the damp wasteland between More Street and the Lose Brook.

Notes

1. VCH, *Essex*, vol. 9, p. 1.

2. ERO, D/B5 Cr75, m. 10r (transcript, p. 59). Middle Mill is just north of the boating lake in the lower Castle Park. When the river is high this area is still prone to inundation.

3. BL, MS Cotton Nero D viii, cited in J. Caley, H. Ellis & B. Bandinel, eds., *W. Dugdale, Monasticon Anglicanum*, vol. 4b, London 1846, p. 607.

4. *civitatem in orientali parte Brittaniae posita; civitas vicina portui, situ ameno, fontibus undique scaturientibus irrigua; aere saluberrimo, moenibus firmissimis constructa.*

5. ERO, D/B5 Cr72, m. 1v (transcript, p. 6).

6. ERO, D/B5 Cr79, m. 17r (transcript, p. 68).

7. See, for example, ERO, D/B5 Cr81, m. 13r (transcript, p. 43), where 'Dodelliswell' is also mentioned.

8. An undated rental (C14th –C15th) for Head Ward refers to the 'Berestake' and to 'Berstake Well' (B.*OB*, p. 211). See below chapter 8: 'Bearbaiting'.

9. Britnell R. H., *Colchester in the Fifteenth Century – a Portrait* (http://www.dur.ac.uk/r.h.britnell/Portrait%203htm), citing ERO, D/B5 Cr26, m. 2r; Cr 31 m. 11r; Cr 36, mm. 6v, 7r.

10. This church, generally known since the Reformation as 'St Mary's', is called 'Our Lady-at-the-Walls' in some

mediaeval documents.

11.   ERO, D/B5 Cr74, m. 1v (transcript, p. 5).

12.   ERO, D/B5 Cr75, m. 10r (transcript, p. 61).

13.   ERO, D/B5 Cr75, m. 10r, 19r (transcript, pp. 61, 103).

14.   ERO, D/B5 Cr77, m. 11v (transcript, p. 56).

15.   ERO, D/B5 Cr75, m. 7v (transcript, p. 43).

16.   ERO, D/B5 Cr 72, m. 1v (transcript, p. 8).

17.   ERO, D/B5 Cr 74, m. 14r (transcript, p. 54).

18.   North ward in the north-west, East ward in the north-east, South ward in the south-east and Head ward in the south-west.

19.   ERO, D/B5 Cr74, m. 29r (transcript, p. 99).

20.   ERO, D/B5 Cr76, m. 2r (transcript, p. 8); Cr77, m. 2r (transcript, p. 6).

21.   ERO, D/B5 Cr77, m. 17v (transcript, p. 91).

22.   ERO, D/B5 Cr79, m. 39r (transcript, p. 154). This was perhaps in the vicinity of St Leonard's Church.

23.   ERO, D/B5 Cr74, m. 13v (transcript, p. 50).

24.   ERO, D/B5 Cr74, m. 11v (transcript, p. 43). 'More Elm Lane' was presumably named for this tree and for More Street (modern Priory Street).

25.   ERO, D/B5 Cr78, m. 15v (transcript, p. 72).

ST JOHN'S ABBEY

Among the most notable lost features of mediaeval Colchester are the town's great religious institutions of which hardly a trace now remains above ground level. At the beginning of the 16th century, just before the Reformation, Colchester had five established religious houses of various types, belonging to different religious orders. These five houses were St John's Abbey (Benedictine monks), St Botoph's Priory (Augustinian canons regular), the Franciscan Priory (Greyfriars), the Priory of the Crossed Friars of St Augustine (previously the Hospital of the Holy Cross) and the Hospital of St Mary Magdalen. It has become the common habit in England to refer to such institutions as 'monasteries' but this is inaccurate and misleading. Houses of friars and canons are not monasteries but convents. The distinction between monasteries and convents depends not (as is popularly imagined) upon the gender of the inhabitants, but upon the nature of the religious rule they observe. Convents are more open to the outside world; monasteries, on the other hand, are more enclosed. In fact mediaeval Colchester had only one true monastery: St John's Abbey. A better global term for such institutions (and the one which is employed here) is 'religious houses'.

With the exception of the leper hospital of St Mary Magdalen, all of Colchester's mediaeval religious houses seem to have disappeared quite quickly following their dissolution by Henry VIII. Even at St Botolph's Priory, where the nave was preserved because it served as a parish church, the conventual choir and domestic buildings vanished entirely. Thus, although the early 17th-century antiquarian John Weever includes mention of Colchester in his *Funeral Monuments*, his sum total for the town amounts to barely a page of print. Moreover, all his information appears to have been derived from manuscript or published sources. One gains no sense that when Weever visited Colchester, he was able to inspect the standing ruins of any of the religious houses (as he was apparently able to do in other locations). The logical conclusion must be that by the first decade of the 17th century, a mere 70 years after the dissolution, there was scarcely anything left to be seen.

Modern archeologists have not fared much better than Weever. The plan of St Botolph's Priory is well established, and remains of the Priory of the Crossed Friars were recently discovered, but the great Church of St John's Abbey has eluded archaeological probings: its site guessed at, but unconfirmed by so much as a single mediaeval stone *in situ*. Of the Franciscan Priory, only foundations of some unidentified outlying domestic building have so far come to light. In attempting to reconstruct the great, vanished mediaeval monastic and conventual churches of Colchester, one is therefore largely dependent on mediaeval written (and occasionally

St John's Abbey Gatehouse as it is today.

pictorial) sources; on the map-makers and antiquaries of the 17th and 18th centuries (who were sometimes able to see just a little more than is now visible above the ground) and on what has survived of similar buildings elsewhere.

Pride of place amongst Colchester's religious institutions belonged unquestionably to St John's Abbey. The precinct walls and main gate of the abbey still stand. Indeed, the gatehouse, set on rising ground, is an imposing and impressive structure. Nevertheless, St John's Abbey is a lost landmark in three senses. Firstly nothing remains visible on site of either the abbey church or the domestic buildings of the monastery. Secondly the site has been in military ownership for 150 years, making it difficult to access.[1] Finally the construction of Colchester's southern bypass, Southway, in the 1960s, effectively cut off the abbey precinct from the town almost completely, so that a visitor on foot is now very unlikely to come across the abbey casually or by accident. A conscious effort and some determination is required if one is to visit the site today. In the Middle Ages, by contrast, the route to the abbey from the town centre via Schere Gate was probably much frequented.

An abbey is a religious house whose community is presided over by an abbot (in the case of a male community – or an abbess in a female community). St John's Abbey, which was also called 'Colchester Abbey', was founded in 1095 as a house of Benedictine monks: this required that the inmates be male and were to be subject to the sixth-century religious 'rule' ascribed to St Benedict. Traditionally the abbey's founder is named as Eudo de Rie, *dapifer* (high steward) of William I and William II and constable of Colchester Castle, but in actual fact no layman can found an abbey. In the western (Catholic) church, the status of 'abbey' can be bestowed on a religious house only by the pope, and we shall return later to the issue of which pope granted the papal bull that raised the monastic house of St John at Colchester to abbatial rank. Presumably what Eudo actually founded was a Benedictine priory. A priory is the basic form of religious house, consisting of a community bound by vows and usually headed by an elected prior (or prioress): a superior of lower rank than an abbot or abbess.

The site chosen by Eudo for his new foundation lay outside the town walls of Colchester to the south. It was on rising ground, partly separated from the town by the Lose Brook. This site was already occupied by a small, pre-Conquest church dedicated to St John the Baptist, which was then served by a priest called Siric.[2] It was presumably from this pre-existing church that the new abbey derived its dedication to St John. The subsequent abbey church seems to have been popularly

Early 15th-century corbel from St John's Abbey Gatehouse carved with an angel holding the *Agnus Dei* (Lamb of God), symbol of St John the Baptist.

regarded as maintaining a primary dedication to St John the Baptist,[3] although both St John the Baptist and St John the Evangelist were depicted on the abbey's great seal, which suggests either that later generations of Colchester monks were uncertain which St John was intended, or that the community saw their house as dedicated to both saints.

Christian monastic tradition stretches back well beyond the lifetime of St Benedict to those hermits who lived austere, solitary religious lives in Egypt in the early centuries of the Christian era, following religious 'rules' ascribed to St Anthony and St Pachomius. The Antonine religious ideal was austere and solitary, but in the fourth century, when St Basil came to organise Greek monasticism, he followed St Pachomius in preferring as his model

The 19th-century stained glass window depicting St John the Baptist holding his emblem, the *Agnus Dei*, from the Church of St James the Less, Colchester.

community life, with meals, work and prayer all in common. Both the solitary and community models of religious life were known in western Europe before the time of St Benedict. Indeed, when Benedict himself determined to forsake the world he at first chose the life of a solitary in a cave. His later 'rule' comprises a blend of the austerities of the solitary life with the ideal of community living.

St Benedict is thought to have written his 'rule' in about 530, probably at Monte Cassino. He wrote it in the late Latin vernacular current at that period. A copy of his 'rule' was rescued and taken to Rome (where it was deposited in the papal library) when the monastery at Monte Cassino was destroyed by the Lombards in 581. When the monastery at Monte Cassino was restored, Pope Zachary (741–52) returned this unique copy of the 'rule' to that house where it was subsequently destroyed by a fire in 896. Before that happened, however, the Emperor Charlemagne had ordered duplicates to be made and distributed to monasteries throughout his empire for their guidance. The earliest surviving copy of the Benedictine rule today is Codex 914 of the St Gall Library. This was copied from Charlemagne's text for the Abbey of Reichnau.

Benedict's rule consists of 73 chapters, covering the duties of the head of the house, matters of discipline and administration and instructions for community worship. It comprises a mixture of firm regulations and more general guidance. Individual ownership of private property was in general prohibited for members of the order who were strictly subject to the religious discipline of the elected head of their house. The religious ideal of obedience was strongly emphasised. The core of the Benedictine rule, however, has been summarised as the

Page from a Breviary, or prayer book, containing the services of the Divine Office.

combination of 'work and prayer'. The rule stresses the importance of manual labour and arranges time to be devoted to it daily. St Benedict also gave detailed instructions for the regulation of the *Opus Dei*: the Divine Office, or 'hours' of prayer, which his monks were required to observe at regular intervals throughout the day. Benedict's ideal was for every monastery to be self-contained in order to avoid, as far as possible, the need for intercourse with the outer world.

The constitution of each Benedictine monastery is individual but all are based on the rule of the founder. The precise idiosyncrasies of the constitution of St John's Abbey, Colchester, are now unknown. However, the abbey was certainly headed by an abbot, who will ideally have been elected by, and from within, the community, and who (once elected) held office for life.[4] Under the abbot, other officials, also appointed from within the community, would govern specific aspects of monastic life. These officers are the 'obedientiaries' and are headed by the prior who is the abbot's deputy. In an abbey a prior holds office not for life, but at the behest of the abbot.

A mediaeval Benedictine community comprised choir monks and lay brothers. The former were generally of higher social rank or were better educated, and their names were prefixed by the title 'Dom' (or in mediaeval English 'Dan') – being an abbreviation for the Latin *dominus* ('lord'). It was the choir monks who had the right to elect the abbot.

Benedictine monks are bound firstly by a vow of *stabilitas*, which is a commitment to remain in the religious house in which they make their profession. Thus they do not normally move from house to house within their order. They are further bound by vows of conversion of manners (covering chastity, poverty and the renunciation of personal possessions) and of obedience to their monastic superior and to the rule.

The history of the Benedictine order in England is a very long one, which begins long before the foundation of the abbey in Colchester and which long outlasts that abbey's dissolution by Henry VIII, reaching down to the present day. St Augustine, who was sent by Pope Gregory the Great to evangelise England in 597, had previously been a monk at the pope's own monastery in Rome.[5] Thus, Augustine brought not only Christianity but also the Benedictine monastic rule to England. In the course of the seventh century, inspired by what they saw at St Augustine's monastery at Canterbury, St Wilfrid and St Benet Biscop founded further English monastic houses along similar lines. Although these early English monasteries were destroyed by Viking invaders in the ninth century, they were the inspiration for the subsequent English monastic tradition, and later monasteries claim moral continuity with them, thus

A Benedictine monk.

making the English Benedictine Congregation the oldest of the 21 Benedictine congregations existing in the Catholic Church today.[6]

Clear continuity can be traced from the present-day congregation back to the English monastic houses restored by St Dunstan, St Ethelwold and St Oswald in the 10th century. These houses were the first to bind themselves into a single congregation by means of a document known as the *Regularis Concordia* or Rule of Agreement. The new Benedictine monastery in Colchester was therefore from the outset a part of the English Benedictine Congregation, though that congregation was formally erected by the Holy See only in the 13th century.

We will digress very briefly at this point to review the subsequent history of Benedictine monasticism in England.

From the 10th to the 16th century the black monks of St Benedict played an integral part in the religious, social and economic aspects of English life. Under King Henry VIII the congregation nearly came to extinction with the dissolution of the monasteries in the 1530s. Queen Mary I took the ancient royal Abbey of Westminster, refounded by King Edward the Confessor in the 11th century, and restored it to a surviving band of monks on 21 November 1556. However, this revival ceased on the accession of Elizabeth I in 1558. By 1607 only one monk of the pre-Reformation congregation survived, Dom Sigebert Buckley. On 21 November 1607 he aggregated two young English monks of the Cassinese Congregation to the English Congregation, thus ensuring a moral continuity of the link to St Augustine.[7]

In the 19th century Benedictine monasteries were re-established in England by members of the English Benedictine Congregation returning from the European mainland. The earliest of these, and the present mother-house of the English Benedictine Congregation, is Downside Abbey in Somerset.

Reputedly, the foundation of Eudo de Rie's Benedictine monastery in Colchester was undertaken in response to a miracle. Eudo obtained the support of the bishop of London for his project and by the late summer of 1096 the plan for his proposed monastic buildings had been marked out on the intended site. However, despite this promising start, building work was not in fact begun until the following Easter and seems to have proceeded at a very leisurely pace. The first monastic buildings were finally completed by 1115. These lay to the north of Siric's original church (i.e on the side towards the town) because the ground to the south was hilly. They will have included a cloister garth: a square enclosure surrounded by covered walkways, reserved for the use of the religious, and around which the domestic buildings of the religious house (sleeping accommodation, refectory and so on) were usually disposed. In 1133 the monastery, in common with much of Colchester, was seriously damaged in a fire. It is reported that the hill was then levelled and the residential buildings moved to the south because the northern side of the abbey had proved too noisy. Nevertheless it seems certain that the cloisters and chapter house always remained on the north side of the church. The sole surviving mediaeval drawing of the abbey

Norman-carved stone from St John's Abbey.

St John's Abbey Church, Colchester, seen from the south.

church, which shows the building viewed from the south, indicates no other buildings attached to it on that side. However, it is also the case that the later mansion built on the abbey site by the Lucas family was depicted on maps as standing to the south-west of the scant ruins of the abbey church which then remained, and directly south of the abbey gatehouse.[8] Such post-Dissolution residences on the sites of religious houses were generally constructed using some of the former domestic buildings of the religious house as their core. It is therefore likely that at St John's Abbey the abbot's lodging, at least, stood to the south-west of the church from the 13th to the 16th centuries in the same general area as the later Lucas mansion. Standing thus somewhat to the south-west, it would have neither adjoined nor obstructed the view of the abbey church on the southern side.

Like the work on the monastic buildings, the establishment of a community of monks in the new foundation proceeded somewhat slowly and suffered various setbacks. At first the bishop of Rochester sent two Benedictine monks from his diocese to Colchester, but these men stayed only a short time before becoming discontented and returning home. Possibly they were dissatisfied at the incomplete state of the buildings. A slightly larger contingent of replacement monks was subsequently dispatched, apparently under the leadership of a man named Ralph. The fact that Ralph reportedly negotiated with Eudo for sources of income to be assigned to the new monastery suggests that until that point no proper financial provision had been made by the founder, and this may well have been an additional reason why the first monks had preferred to return home.

Ralph has some claim to be listed as the first superior of the monastery. His name does not, however, head the list of abbots of Colchester. This may simply be because in his time papal authorisation for Eudo's new foundation to enjoy the rank and status of an abbey had not yet been obtained, so that Ralph was merely prior of Colchester and never abbot. Alternatively, it may be that the eventual decision on the part of Ralph and his monks to follow their predecessors in abandoning Colchester and returning home meant that later generations saw Ralph merely as a kind of false start.

The final, effective foundation of the Benedictine community of Colchester was undertaken by Abbot Stephen of York, who selected 13 monks from his own house and sent them south to Essex. At the same time Eudo seems to have redoubled his efforts to complete the monastic buildings and render them habitable. About the same time a petition must have been addressed to the Holy See requesting abbatial status for the new monastery. This petition was probably granted by Pope Pascal II (1099–1118), himself a former Cluniac monk.[9] Unquestionably the Colchester foundation had been recognised as an abbey by 1104, for in that year the monks from York elected one of their number, named Hugh, as the first abbot of Colchester. Hugh was formally consecrated abbot by the bishop of London. At this stage Colchester was not yet a mitred abbey.[10] It was not until 25 February 1399 that Pope Boniface IX licensed the abbot to wear a mitre and to give solemn blessings at the end of mass and vespers.

Once it was fully functional the community of Colchester Abbey comprised some 20 choir monks, not to mention lay brothers, servants and guests. Of necessity the buildings and grounds were extensive with the immediate precincts of the abbey consisting of grounds extending for about 13 acres. This land was enclosed to the north by a stone-built precinct wall fronting on to St John's Green and Stanwell Street. To the east the same stone wall continued, adjacent to the road which led to Mersea. From the 12th century onwards in the north-eastern corner in front of the main abbey precinct a 'D' shaped extension to the wall formed a 'barbican', which enclosed the parish Church of St Giles.[11] The latter is still extant (though considerably altered over time) and now houses Colchester's Freemasons. This Church of St Giles belonged to, and was served by, the abbey which, almost alone among the religious houses of mediaeval Colchester, exercised no parochial functions at its main (abbey) church.[12] The stone precinct wall also extended along the abbey perimeter on the western side, where this wall now adjoins Flagstaff Road. In the Middle Ages, however, no road existed in this area and the western abbey wall gave out onto fields.

There seems to have been no stone wall enclosing the abbey precincts on the southern side, beyond which lay open country. The principal abbey gateway overlooked St John's Green, facing towards Colchester. Built on high ground the abbey church rising above its precinct walls must have been readily visible from the town.

After the fire of 1133 the abbey church was rebuilt on a cruciform (cross-shaped) plan. This design was used for many mediaeval churches, particularly those which were of some size or considered to be important. The layout comprised a kind of large hall called the *nave* at the western end of the building and a *choir* and *sanctuary* to the east. The choir was where the members of the resident religious community stood or sat to sing during services. The eastern end of the choir formed the sanctuary where the main (or 'high') altar stood at which Mass was celebrated. The arms of the cross shape were formed by north-south projecting wings called 'transepts'. The point at which the east-west wing (nave and choir) met the north-south wing (transepts) was known for obvious reasons as the 'crossing', and above this rose the central tower of the church. Although tentative in respect of precise measurements, the plan of Colchester's abbey church published here will help to make the layout of the building clear.

It was this new, cruciform structure that constituted the basis of the building which is depicted in the only surviving illustration of Colchester's abbey church. It is, of course, very useful to have a surviving representation of the abbey church since the building has entirely vanished. Nevertheless, this little illustration presents certain difficulties. Usually the western part of a church (the nave) was flanked at ground-floor level by pillars and arches within. Beyond these were side extensions, somewhat resembling corridors or passageways, called *aisles*. Above the pillars and arches there was an upper storey containing windows to let light into the nave. This was known as the *clerestory*. Strangely, the surviving depiction of Colchester's abbey church does not appear to show any aisles. However, the church almost certainly did have them. There is obviously a clerestory shown in the picture, but possibly we also need to imagine a *triforium*, or third storey, with smaller windows above the clerestory, although this is not depicted in the drawing.

The church seems to have had two low western towers, while the central crossing was surmounted by a much larger, but fairly short, square tower above which rose a cylindrical *lantern* topped off with a squat spire. In this context a lantern means a circular or polygonal area high in the tower, consisting chiefly of windows designed to light the area of the central crossing in the church beneath.

Tentative reconstructed plan of St John's Abbey Church, Colchester

A	cloister garth	F	transepts
B	west door	G	nave chapel
C	aisles	H	choir
D	nave	I	lady (?) chapel
E	central crossing	K	altar
		L	? chapter house ?

Conjectural plan of St John's Abbey Church.

The nave of Colchester's abbey church apparently had seven *bays* (pairs of arches on either side of the nave). This is quite short for an English mediaeval abbey church, but the nave of the abbey church of the Holy Cross and St Lawrence at Waltham (also in Essex) is likewise seven bays in length. It may be that reconstructions of Waltham Abbey Church as it was in the 12th century (before its choir was first greatly extended, then demolished entirely during the Reformation) help to give us some idea of the size and appearance of the abbey church in Colchester.

At Waltham the length of the nave is 107ft (32.6 m), the transepts and central crossing measured 22ft (6.7m) from west to east and the 12th-century east end (later

Reconstruction of Waltham Abbey Church *c.*1150.

vastly enlarged) was 132ft (40.3m) in length, giving a total length for the church of something in excess of 261ft (79.6m). This total length included an apsidal chapel to the east of the sanctuary. An apsidal chapel has a half-round or polygonal end rather than a squared-off end.

No such apsidal chapel is shown in the surviving representation of Colchester Abbey. Instead, the Colchester church had a squared-off east end in which there was an east window of four lancets (tall, thin, pointed arches). This window probably stood immediately behind (east of) the high altar. At St John's Abbey the eastern arm seems to have been very similar in its dimensions to the nave. It certainly appears to have been shorter than the corresponding eastern arm at Waltham. This suggests that St John's Abbey Church may have totalled something like 240 - 250ft (73.2 - 76.25m) in length, measured from west to east.

The size of the abbey church in Colchester was clearly limited by the space available, for although the foundations of the building have not as yet been found it is believed to have stood south and east of the surviving gatehouse. In this position the line of the precinct wall to the east (along Mersey Road) would not permit the church to exceed a maximum measurement of 300ft (91.5m) in length. In fact, the land closest to the eastern precinct wall may well have been sloping or unstable so that effectively Colchester's abbey church would have needed to be shorter than

300ft. As for its north-south dimensions, at Waltham Abbey the total interior breadth of the nave and aisles is 55ft (16.75m) and we shall see later that the interior measurement of St Botolph's Priory in Colchester is almost identical. It therefore seems likely that St John's Abbey Church was of a similar size.[13]

At a later date side chapels were built onto the southern side of both the nave and the choir at Colchester.[14] Once again there is an analogy here with Waltham Abbey where a single side chapel was later added to the south of the nave. The reason why *two* lateral chapels were added to Colchester's abbey church was presumably because the size limitations of the Colchester site prohibited any eastward expansion of the building (see p.39). Thus, the chapel added to the south of the choir in Colchester would have roughly corresponded to the eastern apsidal chapel at Waltham Abbey – there being no room to extend the church eastwards on the restricted Colchester site.

At Waltham, the chapel added to the south side of the nave (which measures 41ft 6in [12.6m] from east to west and 21ft [6.4m] from north to south) was a lady chapel, and it is probable that one of the side chapels at Colchester fulfilled a similar

Early 15th-century vaulting from St John's Abbey Gatehouse.

The upper room of the
Abbey Gatehouse,
arranged for a
celebration of Vespers for
the Dead in August 2007.

function. It is certain that St John's Abbey housed an image of the Blessed Virgin Mary for the household accounts of John, Lord Howard, Duke of Norfolk (*c*.1422–1485) record that he venerated and made offerings to such an image at the abbey in Colchester. Also an endowment for a perpetual votive light burning before the abbey church's image of the Blessed Virgin existed in the 15th century. This was funded out of the income from a tenement at the Hythe which had been left to the abbey by Robert de Wykes.[15] However, the Blessed Virgin of Colchester Abbey enjoyed no special cult status never acquiring a miraculous reputation, as several similar images did elsewhere.

Evidently the building work at Colchester continued for some time as Henry III gave the abbey 15 oaks in 1235. Around 1170 the new abbey church received its most important relic donated by Ralph, a monk from Canterbury, who had stayed for a time at St John's Abbey during the exile abroad of Archbishop Thomas Becket. When

Early 15th-century vaulting from St John's Abbey Gatehouse.

he returned to Canterbury he was one of those present when Archbishop Becket was murdered. On that occasion Ralph collected a small sample of the martyred archbishop's blood in a glass phial, which he sealed with wax. This was the precious relic which he sent to the Benedictine community at St John's Abbey. Reports of a miracle associated with this relic subsequently found their way back to Canterbury, for although the phial had contained only a few drops of blood when it was sent, on arrival in Colchester it was found to be full to overflowing. Miracles of healing were later attributed to the Colchester relic of St Thomas Becket's blood. However, the abbey never became a significant focus of pilgrimage.

By the 13th century the abbot of Colchester and his community seem to have lost touch somewhat with the Benedictine ideal. There were conflicts between the abbey and the town, particularly in relation to Greenstead and Donyland (where the abbey held the lordship of the manors). In 1272 this conflict led to a riot at the Midsummer fair. There were also disputes, sometimes violent, between the abbey and neighbouring St Botolph's Priory. At his episcopal visitation of the abbey in 1310 Bishop Baldock found that not everything at St John's was as it should have been, and he gave orders that St Benedict's rule should be properly respected regarding periods of silence, abstinence from meat (except in cases of sickness) and the rule of *stabilitas* (whereby monks who made their profession at Colchester should not subsequently be sent to other houses).

Building repairs were undertaken in 1363 and also in the 14th or 15th centuries, at which period the side chapels were added to the nave and chancel of the abbey church. Possibly as a result of the Peasant's Revolt of 1381 the abbey strengthened its defences, making repairs and additions to its precinct wall. The surviving abbey gatehouse was erected soon after this time, probably in the first decades of the 15th century. It constituted the principal (though probably not the only) entrance to the abbey precinct.

The abbey was now becoming involved in politics at a national level. Abbot Geoffrey Story favoured the cause of Richard II. When this king was deposed by his cousin, Henry of Lancaster (Henry IV), the abbot became involved with the countess of Oxford and others who were backing a plot to restore Richard II to the throne. Richard was in fact already dead (possibly starved to death). However, a pretender emerged claiming to be the ex-king and the abbot of Colchester became one of his supporters. When the plot was discovered, St John's Abbey was sequestered by the new king and committed to the safe keeping of the archbishop of Canterbury. There was a full investigation and although the abbot was eventually pardoned, it emerged that other members of the Colchester community had also been implicated in the plot.

Subsequently the abbey continued to harbour anti-Lancastrian sentiments throughout the 15th century. By the 1460s it was closely linked with Sir John Howard (later Lord Howard and Duke of Norfolk), Constable of Colchester Castle, a prominent supporter of the new Yorkist king and owner of a house in Colchester. Howard is known to have exerted some influence during the abbatial election which followed the death of Abbot Ardeley in 1464 in order to secure the election of Abbot John Canon. Canon's abbacy was short: he died in 1468. However, it is probable that Howard subsequently supported the election of Abbot Stansted, whom the earl of Warwick (a Yorkist-turned-Lancastrian) evidently viewed as politically suspect. Howard himself took sanctuary at St John's Abbey during the brief Lancastrian restoration of 1470–71.

St John's
Abbey Gate.

St John's Abbey Gatehouse before the roof and parapet were damaged in the Civil War. This engraving shows the gatehouse almost in its original state. Only the statues in the three niches are missing. Those to the left and right represented respectively St John the Baptist and St John the Evangelist. The statue in the upper niche may have depicted the Holy Trinity or the Virgin Mary.

A carved stone from St John's Abbey thought to date from the 14th century.

Distinguished visitors to the abbey at this period probably included the teenaged Richard, Duke of Gloucester, (the future Richard III) in about 1467.[16] After the deaths of Richard III and John Howard (by then duke of Norfolk) at the Battle of Bosworth in 1485, Richard's friend Francis, Viscount Lovell and other prominent Yorkists took sanctuary at the abbey from whence they attempted to foment rebellion against the new king, Henry Tudor (Henry VII). It is also possible that Richard of Shrewsbury, Duke of York, the younger of the two sons of Edward IV and Elizabeth Woodville (popularly known as 'the princes in the Tower'), was given shelter at the abbey after the accession of Henry VII, his identity concealed in order to protect him.[17]

Colchester Abbey was a very safe place of refuge because it was a chartered sanctuary and the protection it could offer to fugitives was identical to that offered by Westminster Abbey. All churches in England were in some sense places of sanctuary, offering limited protection to men and women escaping the law or other kinds of pursuit. However, in most cases the degree of protection offered was very circumscribed. Colchester Abbey, by contrast, was one of the very few religious houses which held a royal charter granting it special and very extensive rights of sanctuary. This charter was renewed in the mid-15th century by King Henry VI at the specific request of Abbot Ardeley. The king defined the geographical extent of the sanctuary very precisely to extend throughout the entire abbey precinct.

The pro-Yorkist sympathies of Colchester Abbey were maintained, as we have seen, into the Tudor period. As a consequence, the first Tudor king, Henry VII, may have regarded the abbey with some suspicion. However, the dowager Duchess of York (mother of Edward IV and Richard III, and grandmother of Henry VII's queen, Elizabeth of York) remembered the abbey with gratitude and affection and made indirect provision for a bequest in her will.[18] Henry VII may well have stayed at the abbey when he came to Colchester, and there is no doubt whatsoever that his daughter-in-law Catherine of Aragon (the first wife of Henry VIII) did so in 1515.

When Henry VIII discarded Catherine and embarked on the Dissolution of the Monasteries, St John's Abbey was one of only a handful of religious houses that resisted the king. Clearly whatever backslidings there may have been in the past, by this time St John's was fully in touch with its religious heritage. The house was eventually closed following the trial and execution of the last abbot Thomas Beche (*alias* Marshall) for treason.

Doorway to the gatekeeper's lodge.

Doorway in St John's Abbey Gatehouse.

He was hanged at Colchester on the demesne lands of his own abbey on 1 December 1539.[19] The beautiful gold and enamelled pectoral cross which he was wearing at the time of his execution was taken by one of the guards. It subsequently found its way into the hands of the Catholic Mannock family of Gifford's Hall, Stoke-by-Nayland, whose descendants presented this relic to Buckfast Abbey in Devon with the proviso that the abbot of Buckfast should return it to Colchester if and when St John's Abbey was restored.[20]

After the Dissolution, the abbey site passed to various individuals and

Fifteenth-century corbel for the vaulting in the Abbey Gatehouse.

was eventually acquired by the Lucas family who constructed a mansion (probably using the abbot's house as a basis) and resided there until the mid-17th century. They demolished most of the abbey church and used some of the stonework to rebuild Bourne Mill. During the Siege of Colchester in 1648 the former abbey was used as a royalist outpost and sustained considerable damage in the fighting. The gatehouse in particular was targeted by parliamentarian troops whose cannon fire took off the top of the upper storey. With the exception of the gatehouse (which was initially restored after the fighting was over with a pitched roof) the remaining abbey buildings seem to have been demolished in the 1660s. In the 1840s the top of the gatehouse was restored to what appears to be a faithful copy of its original 15th-century design as depicted in the pre-Civil War engraving.

There remains one further interesting point to be explored in respect of St John's Abbey Church: the fact that it may have possessed a large weight-driven clock. The date of the mechanical clock's invention is not precisely known, but by the 13th century attempts were being made to use clockwork mechanisms for telling the time.[21] By about 1300 the eastern counties had certainly produced at least one clockmaker[22] and there is clear evidence to show that in the 15th century there was a clockmaker working in Colchester, a town which would later become famous for its clocks.

The earliest clocks were often constructed in churches. This was partly because they were large mechanisms which required a tower to house them, but it was also because a clock was particularly necessary in a church (and especially in the house of a religious community) for summoning the inhabitants to the daily round of the 'Hours' of prayer. The principal feature of the earliest clocks was that they rang a

The Gateway of St John's Abbey, Colchester.
Publish'd by W. Kymer, Colchester.

St John's Abbey Gatehouse in the early 19th century showing the pitched roof installed after damage during the Civil War.

bell on the hour. The addition of a dial and hour hand (later supplemented by a minute hand) in order to provide a visual signal of the passage of time were later developments.

Was it perhaps, therefore, the presence in Colchester of the rich and powerful St John's Abbey that first attracted to the town its earliest clockmakers? In 1357–58 a man named John Orlogeer was admitted a burgess of Colchester, and later, in 1368–69, William Orlogeer was likewise admitted.[23] Since *horloger* is the French for 'clockmaker' it is possible that John and William were engaged in this profession and may have worked for the abbot of Colchester. At the very least both men must have come from clockmaking families. They also both probably came from the mainland of Europe, possibly from what is now north-eastern France.

We know for certain that there was a clockmaker working in Colchester in the second half of the 15th century because he twice repaired the clock of Sir John, Lord Howard (later Duke of Norfolk). In March 1482 Lord Howard paid 2s 4d 'to the clokke maker of Kolchester for emendyng the clokke'.[24] On that occasion the clockmaker's name was not mentioned. However, he had received 4d for similar services a year earlier when his name was recorded as Wegayn.[25] We can therefore identify him as Austyn Wogayn, who is listed as a 'foreigner' in the register of Colchester inhabitants who did fealty to the restored Edward IV in 1472.[26] The name Wegayn (or Wogayn) is unusual but it could perhaps be an attempt by an

Mediaeval tower clock mechanism from Ramsey Church, now at Colchester Clock Museum.

English-speaking clerk to represent the Flemish surname Begeyn or one of its variants.[27]

In addition, the churchwarden's accounts for Saffron Walden record that during the year 1460–61 the church clock was repaired by a 'man of Colchester' at a cost of 3s. 4d.[28] It seems probable that the man in question was again Austyn Wogayn. Furthermore, we have evidence of the existence of at least two mechanical clocks of 15th-century date in the Colchester area. One stood in the church tower at Ramsey (near Harwich) until the 1950s and is now preserved in Colchester's Clock Museum. The second example was an automaton clock which stood in the tower of the Church of St Leonard at the Hythe.[29] The existence of these two tower clocks, together with the written evidence from Saffron Walden

and from the Howard accounts, clearly indicates the presence of at least one active clockmaker in Colchester in about the third quarter of the 15th century. However, since this man mended, but did not apparently construct, the tower clock at Saffron Walden, he cannot have been the first Essex clockmaker. It therefore seems plausible that the impetus for the development of clockmaking in Colchester may have come initially from the town's abbey.

Corbel from the Abbey Gatehouse, possibly intended to show the head of St John the Baptist on a charger.

Abbots of St John's Abbey

1104	Hugh of York	
?	Gilbert de Lungrill	
*c.*1129	William de Scuri	
*c.*1132	Hugh de Haya	
*c.*1148	Gilbert de Wicham	
*c.*1164	Walter Walensis	
*c.*1179	Osbert	
*c.*1195	Adam de Campes	
1238	William de Wande	
1245	William de Spaldwic	
1272	Robert de Grenstede	
1306	John de Bruges	
1311	Walter de Huntingfeld	
1326	William de Glemham	
1327	John de Wymondham	
1349	Simon de Blyton	
1353	Thomas Moveron	
*c.*1358	Simon	
1368	Thomas Stukelee	
1369	Richard de Colne	
1375	John Dedham	
1377	William de Gritton	
1380	Geoffrey Story de St Osith	

Denton

1405	Roger Best
1418	Robert Gryttone
1432	William Ardeley
1464	John Canon
1468	Walter Stansted
1498	William Lyndesey (or Sprowton)
1517	John Stoke
1523	Thomas Barton

Monks of St John's Abbey

Prior Osmund; Walter

Prior Osmund

Robert

Robert de Sakeville

Thomas Stuckele

John Mersey; John Colchestre (or Pak); John Herst; William

William Shipman; Thomas Thursteyn

... Thaxted; (?)Richard 'of the monistory'[30]

1533   Thomas Marshall (or Beche)   Prior John Milford; John Frances (sub-prior); Thomas Tye(or Essex); John Flyngant; Thomas Clare; William Westmynster; John Pepper; William Page; John Islipp; William Ros; Henry Bumstede; William Ryppnere; John Franceys; George Dedham; Thomas Stow; Sylvester Hynygam; Robert Reason

Notes

1. The abbey site was bought by the War Office in 1860 from the Baring family.

2. The foundations of this pre-Conquest church were discovered in the 1970s.

3. It is described as the Church of St John the Baptist in the court rolls: ERO, D/B5 Cr79, transcript, p. 5.

4. The realities governing elections of mediaeval abbots are explored in more detail below.

5. Pope Gregory I was himself a Benedictine monk before his election as pontiff.

6. At the present day the English Benedictine Congregation comprises 10 abbeys of monks and 3 abbeys of nuns.

7. Website of the English Benedictine Congregation: www.benedictines.org.uk

8. See D.J. Gamble, *St Giles's Church*, Colchester 1998, p. viii for illustrations.

9. No record of the grant of abbey status to Colchester seems to be extant in England. It is possible that some record remains among the Vatican Archives but these are notoriously difficult to search as there is no comprehensive index.

10. Some, but not all, abbots are authorised by the pope to wear a mitre, like a bishop.

11. So called by Henry VI when he defined the extent of the abbey's rights of sanctuary.

12. The only other religious foundation in Colchester whose church was not parochial was that of the Greyfriars.

13. Dimensions for Waltham Abbey are taken from *RCHM*, vol. 2, 1921, pp. 238–42. The transepts at Waltham do not survive, but the west wall of the south transept suggests that this transept, at least, measured 31ft 6in (9.6m) from the central crossing to the south wall.

14. The available evidence does not indicate whether any chapels also adjoined the north aisle, but the available space would have been limited as we must allow for the cloister.

15. ERO, D/B5 Cr77, m. 6v (transcript, p. 29). The tenement stood on the south side of *Hethestrete* (modern Hythe Hill).

16. The future Richard III certainly came to Colchester in either 1467 or 1468, and was probably accommodated at the abbey: J. Ashdown-Hill, 'Yesterday my Lord of Gloucester came to Colchester', *Essex History*, 2005.

17. See D. Baldwin, *The Lost Prince*, Stroud 2007.

18. The duchess made her clandestine bequest to the abbey *via* her servant, Richard Lessy: TNA, PROB 11/11 (image reference 310), will of Richard Lessy.

19. The abbey had a gallows at its manor of Greestead and that may be where Abbot Beche was executed. A contemporary illustration of his execution shows rising ground in a rural setting overlooking the town, Greestead would fit this picture.

20. It qualifies as a relic since Abbot John Beche was beatified (proclaimed 'Blessed') by Pope Leo XIII on 13 May 1895.

21. E. Bruton, *The History of Clocks and Watches*, London 1979, p. 32.

22. A seal of *c.*1300, recently found in York, is inscribed *Sigillum Roberti Horologiarii de Ierm.* ('The seal of Robert the Clockmaker from Yarmouth'): *Current Archaeology*, no. 215 (February 2008), p. 5.

23. B. Mason, *Clock and Watchmaking in Colchester, England*, London 1969, p. 43.

24. Soc. Ant., MS 76, f. 119v; *HHB*, part 2, p. 167.

25. Soc. Ant., MS 76, f. 45r; *HHB*, part 2, p. 49.

26. See appendix 2.

27. I am grateful to Revd Erwin Lammens, Vicar of Dovercourt, for this suggestion.

28. '*Item solut pro reparacione orlogij homini de Colchester, ijs. iiijd.*' Saffron Walden Churchwarden's Accounts, 1439–90, f. 61, cited in Mason, *Clock and Watchmaking in Colchester*, p. 43.

29. Mason, *Clock and Watchmaking in Colchester*, pp. 47–50.

30. ERO, D/B5 Cr75, m. 6v (transcript, p. 34). A person of this name is mentioned in 1473/4 as having formerly owned land at West Donyland, but it is not certain that he was a choir monk. He could have been a lay brother, or even an employee at the abbey.

THE TWO PRIORIES

In addition to its great Benedictine Abbey, Colchester was also home to two priories: St Botolph's Priory and the Franciscan Priory (Greyfriars). The first of these was St Botolph's Priory, which we may best describe as a partially lost mediaeval landmark. The priory site, usually approached today from Priory Street, is not difficult to find, and the ruins of the nave of the priory church still stand to a height of two storeys – albeit in a fragmentary state. Of the transepts and choir of the church, however, nothing remains visible except for some modern concrete mounds and lines on the ground which indicate the positions of the lost walls and columns. As for the cloister and the domestic buildings of the priory, together with its gatehouse, these features have completely vanished, though the 19th-century Church of St Botolph stands on

Reconstruction of St Botolph's Priory Church in the snow seen from the south-west, from the painting by Peter Froste.

the site of the south range of the cloister. The priory site is now somewhat hidden from the road, although in the Middle Ages the Norman facade of its impressive church would have been clearly visible from the king's highway just outside Colchester's South Gate (St Botolph's Gate).

At St Botolph's Priory in Colchester the religious community comprised a convent of Augustinian canons regular. The canons regular of St Augustine (or 'black canons' as they are also called) are priests who share a community life, bound by rules of obedience, chastity and common property, according to the rule of St Augustine of Hippo (354–430). Canons regular are neither monks nor friars.[1] In the Middle Ages one factor which distinguished canons from the other types of male religious order then in existence was the fact that all canons were, by definition, priests. For while monks and friars *may* be priests (and nowadays usually are) they need not be, and in the Middle Ages they frequently were not.

Like a Benedictine monastery, a house of canons regular may be either a priory or an abbey depending on the status of its superior. In the case of St Botolph's in Colchester the head of the house was a prior, so the house was a priory. In

An Augustinian Canon.

principle the mediaeval priors of St Botolph's would have been elected for life, but in practice priors did sometimes resign or were moved elsewhere (since, unlike Benedictine monks, Augustinian canons were not bound by a vow of *stabilitas*, and could be moved to other houses within their order). Thus, for example, on 12 April 1464 John Wardhous is described as 'lately prior of St Botolph's'. However, he was certainly not dead, since he was acting as the executor of a will.[2] Presumably he had resigned from office.

The history of the canons regular can be traced back to the early days of the Christian church, when two categories of priest gradually emerged: those who worked with the bishop and were based at the cathedral church, and those who served other churches. The former were known as *canones* (from the Greek word for 'rule'), the latter were called *vagantes*. Indeed, until modern times the core priests of a cathedral church continued to be known as 'canons'. Gradually, however, some groups of canons moved out of the cathedrals to serve other churches. In the 11th and 12th centuries, as successive popes reformed the life of the clergy, those houses of canons which were not attached to cathedrals were encouraged to accept the rule of St Augustine and, in general, did so with enthusiasm. This was when they became known as 'canons regular' from the Latin *regula* ('rule').

The order of Augustinian canons spread rapidly throughout Europe especially in France, the Low Countries, England and central Europe. In mediaeval England houses of canons outnumbered even the houses of Benedictine monks. Canons regular were known for the splendour of their worship. For this and other reasons, some cathedrals and important places of pilgrimage (such as the shrine of Our Lady of Walsingham in England) were given into their care. The canons also took a leading role in intellectual life, the University of Paris being in part founded by them. In Europe as a whole, Augustinian priories were often sited in towns where their canons served in parish churches and cathedrals, ran hospitals (such as St Bartholomew's, London) or functioned as teachers. In England (where the earliest Augustinian priory was St Botolph's in Colchester) the canons tended to follow a more contemplative lifestyle. The turmoil of the Reformation hit the canons regular very badly, for they lost all of their numerous English houses. Later the French Revolution would deal them further blows. At the present day very few houses of Augustinian canons remain in existence: they are to be found chiefly in Central Europe (Italy, Austria and Switzerland).

The modern parish Church of St Botolph stands beside the ruins of its predecessor, just outside the walls of Colchester and towards the south-eastern corner of the town.

Not much is known about the church's chief patron, St Botolph (whose feast day falls on 17 June). He was an Anglo-Saxon abbot who lived during the second half of the seventh century and is believed to have headed a monastery at Boston (originally 'Botolph's Stone') in Lincolnshire.

Its dedication to an Anglo-Saxon saint indicates that Colchester's original St Botolph's Church must have predated the Norman conquest. It is reputed to have had a tower similar to the surviving Anglo-Saxon tower of Holy Trinity Church inside the town walls.[3] St Botolph's is believed to have been one of many churches throughout the country holding major relics of St Botolph. The church's secondary dedication, to St Julian, may have been a later addition. However, of the several St Julians who are potential candidates for this secondary patronage, all had lived in the early centuries of the Christian era and well before the 11th century. According to some sources the priory also had a third patron: St Denis.[4]

The impetus for the introduction of the Augustinian rule at St Botolph's apparently lay with a priest from Kent called Norman, whose name suggests that he was of Norman rather than Anglo-Saxon origin. During (probably) the 1080s Norman spent some time in France where he studied under Anselm, a learned Italian, who had been elected first prior (1063) and subsequently abbot (1078) of Bec in Normandy. Anselm crossed the Channel to England in 1092, and the following year he was chosen to succeed Lanfranc as archbishop of Canterbury.

Norman also returned to England. Possibly he travelled with Anselm, but at all events he returned at about the same time. He then made his way to Colchester where, at St Botolph's, he joined an already-existing small college of priests who were living together and serving the church as an informal religious community under the leadership of a (presumably) Anglo-Saxon priest called Ainulf. This informal community of priests expressed the desire to join a formal religious order and Norman advised that the order of Augustinian canons regular might be suitable. At that time this order was still unknown in England, so Ainulf sent Norman and another member of their community to Archbishop Anselm who happily approved the plan. The primate sent both men to France to learn the Augustinian rule, which they did in Augustinian houses at Chartres and Beauvais. They then returned to Colchester to pass on what they had learned, and in that way St Botolph's joined the Augustinian order, thus achieving the distinction of becoming the first house of Augustinian canons in England.

The community at St Botolph's must have joined the Augustinian order before August 1100, as King William II (who was killed on 2 August 1100) granted the canons of St Botolph's a charter of protection. We may therefore tentatively date the foundation of the Augustinian priory to about 1099. The display board at the priory site which dates the foundation of the house to 1103 is therefore in error. Ainulf, who had previously headed the secular college of priests at St Botolph's, is named as prior in 1116, and it is very probable that he was elected to this office as soon as the Augustinian priory came into being. The new Augustinian priory was to consist of the prior and 12 canons (in imitation of Christ and his 12 apostles). A benefaction in 1281 allowed this number to be increased by one canon, but the house never grew any larger, and in 1534, when the community formally recognised Henry VIII's new act of succession, only the prior and seven canons were in residence.

Although it was the first, St Botolph's was not the only church served by a college of secular priests to transform itself into an Augustinian priory at about this period. Similar transformations took place elsewhere, for example, at Walsingham in Norfolk and at Waltham Holy Cross in Essex. Like the church at Waltham, the church of the Augustinian community at St Botolph's was destined to remain both a parish church and a priory church until the priory was dissolved by Henry VIII in the 16th century. As a result some clear physical division would have been required between the nave (which constituted the parish church) and the choir (which formed part of the enclosed area reserved for the canons). At Waltham Abbey (and also at the Benedictine abbey of Wymondham in Norfolk, which likewise served both as a parish and a religious community) this physical separation was quite a solid one, consisting of a stone wall which completely closed off the nave at its eastern end. Small doorways towards the northern and southern ends of this wall gave members of the religious order access to the nave so that they might celebrate mass for the parish. It is probable that there was a similar wall across the eastern end of the nave at St Botolph's, completely cutting off the choir and east end of the church from the lay people. At the time of the Dissolution it will have been this vital wall which ensured the preservation of the nave as the parish church. Beyond it the eastern (conventual) part of the church will have been stripped of its roof by the king's commissioners, who will have sold the lead and timber. The roofless choir will then have become a quarry for stone, disappearing rapidly. This explains why only the ruins of the nave (which was wrecked just over a hundred years later during the Civil War) now survive on site above ground level.

The pre-eminence of St Botolph's in terms of the date of its foundation was formally recognised by a bull of Pope Pascal II dated August 1116. The pope

Norman stonework around the 'Pardon Door' (great west door) of St Botolph's Priory Church.

accordingly acknowledged St Botolph's as the mother house of all Augustinian priories of canons in England. In spite of this the Colchester priory was never really able to exercise any authority over the other Augustinian houses in England, most of which were much larger and wealthier establishements. Pope Pascal is also said to have granted special powers for the granting of absolutions by the priory on the feast of St Denis (9 October) and during its octave (the eight days following the feast itself). Morant reports that the Sunday following the feast of St Denis was known as 'Pardon Sunday' in Colchester. There was presumably a popularly perceived connection between the priory's right to grant pardons at this season and Colchester's St Denis fair.[5]

St Botolph's priory had no powerful aristocratic or royal founder. At first the endowments of the house were small but the canons did receive grants from Henry I (1100–1135) and from members of the nobility. As a result, 'by the end of the 12th century their possessions were considerably increased, as recited in a charter of Richard I dated 4 December 1189'.[6] The community had evidently acquired sufficient means to be able to rebuild its church in the Norman-style on a substantial

Norman stonework (detail) around the 'Pardon Door' (great west door) of St Botolph's Priory Church.

Interior of St Botolph's Priory Church viewed from just behind the site of the high altar looking west towards the crossing and nave.

scale. Precisely when this work was started is not on record, but it was presumably finished by 1177 when the new church was dedicated.

With an original total length of just over 176ft (53.7m) from west to east, the mediaeval priory church of St Botolph was about twice the length of the surviving ruins (which, as we have seen, represent only the greater part of the nave).[7] The church was cruciform (cross-shaped) with a central tower and transepts. The length of the nave was 110ft (33.5m) and the breadth of the nave and aisles together was 55ft (16.75m). These dimensions for the western arm of the priory church are very similar to the equivalent measurements at Waltham Abbey, and probably also those at St John's Abbey (see previous chapter). The height of the western gable when intact was probably about 45ft (13.7m). The crossing at St Botolph's measured roughly 24sq ft (7.3m).[8] The church's eastern arm was much shorter than that of St John's Abbey at 42ft (12.8m) long, and it was flanked at its western end by two small side chapels 15ft 6in (4.7m) in length. One of these was undoubtedly the lady chapel, while the other was dedicated either to St Catherine of Alexandria or to St Thomas Becket (see p. 62).

The priory cloisters adjoined the nave on the southern side. In fact, the modern (19th-century) St Botolph's Church stands on the site of the south range of the mediaeval cloister. As for the domestic buildings of the priory, in 1383 the canons' dormitory was in the process of being rebuilt, and in the early 15th century an indulgence was offered to all those who contributed to the refurbishment of the priory buildings.

By 1281 the church had a chapel of St Thomas, and by the beginning of the 15th century, at the latest, there was also a chapel dedicated to St Catherine. Soon afterwards there is mention of a lady chapel next to the choir which was refurbished in 1488. The lady chapel undoubtedly contained an image of the Blessed Virgin Mary, before which burned a perpetual votive light funded by the income from a piece of land at the Hythe which had been left to the priory for this purpose.[9] The benefactor is unknown but may have been Robert de Wykes, who left an adjacent tenement to St John's Abbey in order to fund a similar votive light in the lady chapel there. By the early 16th century there was also a Trinity chapel. The surviving rose window at the west end of the church is believed to be one of the earliest in England and was probably inspired by Chartres Cathedral.

By the late Middle Ages a large church like St Botolph's could be expected to have at least two bells: a smaller *sanctus* bell and a larger bell for tolling at *requiems* (funeral masses or memorial masses for the dead).[10] In fact, St Botolph's Church does indeed seem to have had more than one bell, for the will of William Bonefaunt senior, written on 18 January 1466,[11] requested burial in St Botolph's churchyard and left money to the canons 'for ryngyng of the grete belle and for my absolucion to have at the grete dore' –

Niche from the north range of the cloister of St Botolph's Priory.

The west front of St Botolph's Priory Church with the 'Pardon Door' and rose window.

presumably the central western door of the church, the great Norman archway of which still stands today. Fifty years later in 1514 this entrance was called the 'pardon door' so it evidently had special associations with the granting of absolution and was probably connected with the priory's right to grant pardons at the time of the

St Denis fair (see above). The will's reference to the 'grete belle' implies that there was at least one other bell at the priory. William Bonefaunt also left money to the prior in return for prayers for his soul. It is interesting that Bonefaunt should have chosen to make his bequests to St Botolph's priory, as one member of his family was among the friars at Colchester's Franciscan priory (see below).

St Botolph's Priory never enjoyed great wealth or held extensive landed property. For this reason the prior was much less likely to find himself in dispute with the burgesses of mediaeval Colchester than the far more affluent abbot of St John's was. The chief possessions of St Botolph's Priory around Colchester were in Greenstead (where the priory owned a few rents) and at Cannock (or Canwick – originally 'Canons' Wick') in West Donyland.

Priors of St Botolph's Priory

		Canons of St Botolph's Priory
*fl.*1100–16	Ainulf	Norman of Kent
*fl.*1145	John	
*fl.*1205–06	Henry	
*fl.*1222	Robert	
*fl.*1224–40	Hasculph	
*fl.*1246–59	John	
*fl.*1281	Simon	
*fl.*1290–95	Richard	
?	John de Colum	
*fl.*1323	Richard le Brom	
*fl.*1326–38	John	
d.1361	Thomas Sakkot	
*fl.*1363–64	John	
*fl.*1374–91	John Neylond	
1391–93	John Okham	
*fl.*1393–1412	William Westbrome	
*fl.*1416	William Colchester	
*fl.*1424–34	John Depyng	
*fl.*1437	John	
*fl.*1450	Thomas Colman	
*fl.*1457	John Wardhous	

fl.1462–85(?)	John Flyngaunt	John Maye
fl.1497	John Stampe	John Grew; Richard White
fl.1514	William	
d.1527	William Gooche	
1527–36	Thomas Turner	Robert Bawde; Richard Parker; William Shyrwyn; John Garrard; John Gyppys; Robert Rand; William Patche

Unlike St Botolph's Priory, the Priory of the Franciscan (or Grey) friars is among the most completely lost of all the great landmarks of mediaeval Colchester. Even if they realise the significance of the name 'Greyfriars', most modern Colcestrians probably have little idea what this building might once have looked like. Today it requires a considerable effort of the imagination to visualise, on the Greyfriars site at the top of East Hill, the very large priory church which once stood there crowned with a soaring octagonal belfry and a tall, slender spire. Nevertheless, thanks partly to its impressive site on elevated ground dominating the eastern approaches to the town, this forgotten building must once have been the most notable of Colchester's landmarks. Its tall spire would have been a feature visible for miles around, rather like the clocktower of the town hall is today. Neither St Botolph's Priory (on its low-lying site) nor St John's Abbey (situated off to one side of the town and partly hidden behind the town walls and its own precinct walls) can possibly have rivalled the visual impact of the Franciscan Priory Church, which, in the later Middle Ages, must have been by far the most prominent feature on Colchester's skyline.

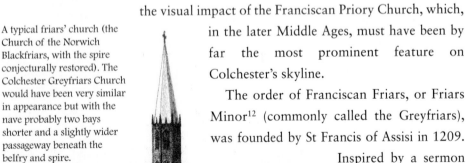

A typical friars' church (the Church of the Norwich Blackfriars, with the spire conjecturally restored). The Colchester Greyfriars Church would have been very similar in appearance but with the nave probably two bays shorter and a slightly wider passageway beneath the belfry and spire.

The order of Franciscan Friars, or Friars Minor[12] (commonly called the Greyfriars), was founded by St Francis of Assisi in 1209. Inspired by a sermon based upon the gospel of St Matthew, chapter 10, verse 9 (in which Christ sends his disciples out to preach without wealth or possessions), Francis decided to devote himself to a life of poverty. Clad in rough clothing and with bare feet he began to preach repentance. He soon acquired a small band of followers and obtained the approval of Pope Innocent III for his community as one of the new orders of friars.

Friars differ from monks and actually more closely resemble canons regular in having more day-to-day contact with the world. They do not live (as monks in principle do) withdrawn in cloistered seclusion. Also, like canons, friars are not tied to one particular convent. Thus they may move (or be moved) from house to house within their order. Friars differ from canons regular in one important point however: they are not, or, at least, were not in the Middle Ages, necessarily priests. In England a house of Franciscan friars normally has the status of a priory, although its elected superior actually bears the title not of prior but of 'guardian'.

Thanks to their commitments to poverty, charitable work and preaching the emerging orders of friars were particularly popular in the 13th century and enjoyed ready support both from wealthy patrons and among the faithful in general.

From an early date dissentions proliferated among the followers of St Francis with the result that the order eventually became fragmented.[13] It was largely in response to early disputes that in 1221 Francis, with the help and advice of Cardinal Ugolino and others, created a formal rule for his friars – subsequently revised slightly in 1223. Meanwhile, despite its internal dissentions, the new order spread rapidly. The Friars Minor of the order of St Francis of Assisi first came to England in about 1224, where they became known as 'Greyfriars' from the colour of their habit.[14] The English province of the Franciscan order was divided into seven administrative areas or wardenships. The Franciscan priory in Colchester formed part of the wardenship of Cambridge together with eight other houses.

St Francis himself died in 1226. He was succeeded as overall head of the order by Brother Elias of

A Franciscan Friar.

Cortona, an able but autocratic leader, who ruled his friars strictly from the centre. This provoked strong reactions in some quarters, most notably in the English and German provinces of the order. So much so that Pope Gregory IX deemed it necessary to preside in person over the general chapter of the Franciscan order held in Rome in 1239. At this meeting Elias was deposed in favor of Albert of Pisa – the former Franciscan provincial of England and a much more moderate man.[15]

The precise origins of the Greyfriars priory in Colchester are not clearly recorded, but the house was an early foundation which came into being as part of the initial rapid spread of the new order. It was already in existence in 1237 when Henry III granted the Franciscan friars of Colchester additional land to enlarge their plot. They had established themselves on the north side of what is now the High Street, between the castle and the town's East Gate. Eventually their land would extend down to the town wall on the northern side giving them a very large precinct. However, friars preferred their houses to be located on or near a main thoroughfare so that they were readily accessible to the populace, so it is therefore probable that the Colchester convent always had its main buildings on the upper (southern) part of the Greyfriars site, adjacent to the modern High Street.

The site of the Franciscan Priory viewed from just inside the northern town wall. All the land from the north wall to St James's Church belonged to the priory.

On 25 January 1279 King Edward I licensed the friars to construct an underground conduit through his demesne lands and meadows, transecting also the town wall, in order to bring water to their house from Coningswell – a well outside the wall, which Nicholas de Warde had given to them. The king's permission was granted on condition that once the conduit was in place the friars should fill in their trenches and repair the town wall at their own cost.[16] It seems likely that the well lay just outside the town wall on the northern side on low-lying land not far from the river. It was therefore located at quite some distance from the domestic buildings of the priory and deep trenches would have been required for the conduit, especially at the upper (southern) end of the pipeline. The friars did not, at this early period, own the intervening land through which the trench for the conduit had to be dug. It was not until almost 150 years later that they managed to acquire it.

At their fullest extent the lands of the Greyfriars enclosure in Colchester filled the entire north-eastern corner of the town, north of what is now the High Street. Indeed, this part of the High Street was formerly known as Frere Street (Friar Street). Their possession of this large plot, between the town walls to the east and north and the grounds of the royal castle to the west, made the Franciscan community unique amongst the religious orders of mediaeval Colchester since theirs was the only religious house *inside* the town walls.

Usually some wealthy patron lay behind the foundation of a new convent of friars. Who first encouraged the Franciscans to come to Colchester is unknown but one of their early patrons, whom they later remembered as their founder, was Robert Fitzwalter. Owing to the later closure of the convent, and the loss of the friars' own records, it may be that some confusion has crept into the story here, for there were two Robert Fitzwalters. The Robert who lived from *c*.1250 to 1325/6 was a man of some importance, being the second cousin of King Edward I with whom he shared a common descent from their mutual great grandfather, Henry II (the founder of the Plantagenet line in England). Fitzwalter's mother, Ida, had been one of the daughters of William Longspee, Earl of Salisbury, an illegitimate son of Henry II, possibly by 'the fair Rosamund' (Rosamund Clifford). In 1295 Edward II created Robert 1st Baron Fitzwalter.[17] Weever, writing in the early 17th century, certainly claimed this Robert Fitzwalter as the founder of the Colchester Greyfriars, citing as his evidence a Latin note in the *Book of Dunmow* among the Cotton manuscripts: 'Friar, Lord Robert Fitzwalter, Baron, founder of the Colchester Convent, entered the same order in the year of the Lord 1325'.[18]

However, since the Colchester convent was already in existence before he was born, it is immediately clear that Lord Fitzwalter cannot have been its first founder. We need to bear in mind the fact that the title of 'founder' in monastic and conventual houses was hereditary, so almost certainly the original impetus for the Colchester Greyfriars' foundation had come from one of Lord Fitzwalter's forebears: either from his father, Sir Walter Fitzrobert (died 1258), or more probably from his identically-named grandfather, Robert Fitzwalter of Dunmow (died 1235). If grandfather Robert was the true founder, it is easy to understand how confusion could later have arisen between his grandson and namesake who became a friar of the convent and was buried there.

We have seen that initially the land granted to the Greyfriars in Colchester was quite limited in its extent. However, there was steady augmentation as two parcels of land were granted to them by Robert Fitzwalter the younger. In 1293 he gave a plot of unspecified size lying to the west of (and adjoining) the Greyfriars' existing holding and in 1309 he added a further half-acre. In the same year another piece of land was granted by John Boteturte. It was probably upon the land granted by their patron that a new

Tentative reconstructed plan of the Franciscan Priory, Colchester

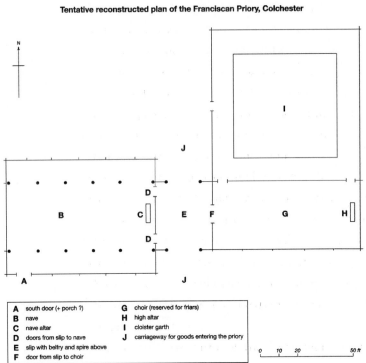

A	south door (+ porch ?)	G	choir (reserved for friars)
B	nave	H	high altar
C	nave altar	I	cloister garth
D	doors from slip to nave	J	carriageway for goods entering the priory
E	slip with belfry and spire above		
F	door from slip to choir		

Conjectural plan of the Franciscan Priory Church, Colchester (Greyfriars), based on the layout of the Blackfriars and the Whitefriars Churches in Norwich.

conventual church was erected and it is also very likely that this was built largely at Fitzwalter's expense. It was in 1325 that Robert himself joined the order as a friar.[19] This was not an uncommon phenomenon. Fitzwalter died later the same year. As (hereditary) founder of the Colchester convent, he was doubtless buried in the friars' newly erected church in a place of honour, perhaps in the choir before the high altar.

Fourteenth-century friars' churches generally followed a consistent overall plan with only minor variations to suit the available plot of land. The church often lay adjacent to a main thoroughfare, encouraging ready access to the nave for the public to hear the friars preach. In the case of the Colchester Greyfriars the church (orientated as usual from west to east) will have lain parallel to Frere Street (modern High Street). The site of its nave may now be partly or entirely covered by the present red-brick Georgian 'Greyfriars' building.[20] This 18th-century structure is approximately 80ft in length measured from its western end to the north-south passageway at the eastern extremity of the building, which leads into the grounds at the rear. This corresponds well with the likely length of such a nave. In the 19th century skeletons were found in the garden to the east of this building and these burials may originally have lain in the east end (choir) of the priory church.

The nave, with its aisles, constituted the western end of the church and as a general rule friars' churches had no transepts.[21] At the eastern end of the nave two doorways, to the right and left of the nave altar, would have led into a 'slip' or passageway transecting the church building from south to north and providing access from the roadway to the courtyard and domestic buildings which lay behind the church to the north. This was a practical measure to allow for deliveries of supplies to the convent. Above the slip rose the slim, octagonal belfry tower and spire which would have made the Greyfriars church such a prominent and instantly recognisable feature of the skyline of mediaeval Colchester.

East of the slip and the tower would have been the friars' choir, a private part of the church completely cut off from the nave by the walls of the slip. Unlike the nave, the choir was not normally accessible to the general public. It was here that, at regular intervals throughout the day, the friars would assemble in their choir stalls to sing the 'hours' of the Divine Office: *matins, prime, lauds, terce, sexte, none, vespers* and *compline* at roughly three-hourly intervals from early morning to late evening. Somewhere in their priory church – and most probably in the choir – the Franciscan friars of Colchester had a pair of organs which were borrowed by Sir John Howard for the Christmas celebrations of 1463.[22] Mediaeval organs were not the huge

The east range of the cloister garth of the Blackfriars priory, Norwich. The cloister of Colchester's Greyfriars would have been very similar in appearance.

instruments seen in churches today. Their keyboards were of similar size to a piano accordion topped by a small bank of pipes some three feet in height. They were therefore readily portable. The pair of organs which Howard had in his own private chapel at Framlingham Castle some years later had four stops each.[23]

The cloister garth of a friars' convent typically adjoined the choir rather than the nave since, as its name indicates, the *cloister* formed part of the religious enclosure. As at all religious houses, the cloister might stand either on the north or the south side of the church depending upon the particular site and layout. In the case of Colchester Greyfriars the cloister will have been situated to the north of the choir,

Surviving fragment of the slip wall? This old masonry survives in a passageway at the eastern end of the modern Greyfriars building.

adjoining its northern wall. Around this cloister stood the friars' domestic buildings. The church itself would have secluded these buildings from the roadway and the only access to them would have been by means of the slip.

Interestingly, it is just possible that part of one of the side walls of the slip still survives, built into the later Georgian 'Greyfriars', as the present passageway through from the street to the car park at the east end of the extant 'Greyfriars' building contains some older masonry. Recent excavations in the car park to the north of Greyfriars have revealed footings of what are most probably domestic buildings: some of those which once surrounded the cloister. A section of the north wall of the present Greyfriars building, together with the north-south wall enclosing the grounds on the western side, probably contains reused stone from the conventual buildings. Otherwise, sadly nothing is now left on the original site to indicate what an impressive church and convent once occupied this commanding site. Nevertheless, the fact that most friars' churches were built to a basically similar plan means we can use the well-preserved church of the Dominican Priory (Blackfriars) in Norwich to help us imagine what Colchester once had.

The Norwich Blackfriars church building totals 252ft in length, of which the nave alone comprises 126ft. This exceeds the likely length of the Colchester Greyfriars nave. A comparison could also be made with the Norwich Whitefriars' church. Although that building is no longer standing, thankfully both Norwich churches were measured in paces by William Worcester in the 15th century. By comparing William's pace length for the Blackfriars with the modern measurement of that building in feet one can deduce the approximate length of William's pace. On this basis the total length of the Norwich Whitefriars church appears to have been about 225ft, with the nave alone comprising about 80ft – similar to the length of the present building on the Colchester Greyfriars site and therefore very possibly the length of the Colchester church's nave. In fact, the Colchester Greyfriars church was perhaps closer in size to the Norwich Whitefriars than to the Blackfriars: 225ft in total length. The Colchester priory church may thus have had five bays to the nave and five bays to the choir (whereas the longer nave of the Norwich Blackfriars church has seven bays).

The dimensions of the component parts of the Norwich Whitefriars church are: nave – 80ft; slip – 40ft and choir – 105ft. The slip at the Whitefriars was much wider than that of the surviving Norwich Blackfriars.[24] It is probable that the arrangements at the Colchester Greyfriars were rather similar to those at the Norwich Whitefriars, because in both cases the slip must have constituted the principal entry to the priory enclosure. It is therefore likely to have been broad enough to allow a cart or wagon to pass through into the courtyard.

In 1338 the Franciscan friars obtained a further plot of land from John Caproun designed to extend the domestic buildings of the priory. Clearly, therefore, the new plot of land lay to the north of the church, perhaps in the vicinity of modern Castle Road. In 1348 more land for the same purpose (and probably in the same general area) was acquired from John le Porcherde.[25] In 1423 the friars purchased 84 acres from John Podde.[26] This land contained the underground conduit which gave them their only water supply. Its acquisition must therefore have extended the northern boundary of the priory precinct right down to the town wall on the northern side.

Details of all the aristocratic patrons of Colchester's Franciscan friars do not survive, but during the Yorkist period the friars enjoyed the patronage of Sir John, Lord Howard, constable of Colchester Castle and eventually duke of Norfolk – that same John Howard who enjoyed close connections with St John's Abbey. On Monday 30 September 1465 Catherine de Moleyns, Lady Howard, Sir John's first wife, gave the not inconsiderable sum of five shillings to the Greyfriars in Colchester.[27] She was already seriously ill at the time and may have realised that she was dying. Another entry in the Howard accounts for the same date records the purchase of medicine for her in Colchester, together with sugar candy, water of honeysuckles and wine (no doubt intended as remedies).[28] More medicine was bought for her the following month on 26 October 1465 in Ipswich.[29] All was in vain, however, and she soon died, probably on Tuesday 12 November. The following day her grieving widower sent 40 shillings to the Colchester Greyfriars in payment for a trental of masses (30 masses) for the repose of her soul.

In March 1469 King Edward IV generously granted to Robert Wotton, guardian of the priory, and to the friars, 52 cartloads of 'underwood' (brushwood) yearly from the forest of Kingswood for use as fuel.[30] In return the friars were to pray for the good estate of the king and his consort during their lifetimes, and subsequently to commemorate the anniversaries of their deaths (together with that of the king's late father, Richard, Duke of York). Each cartload of wood was to be such as could be drawn by six horses or other beasts of burden and the friars were granted free entry into the forest to cut and transport their fuel.

In the 15th century and in the first third of the 16th century (the period immediately preceding the Dissolution) the Greyfriars of Colchester seem to have retained popular support and affection. At this time their priory church housed a guild of the Blessed Virgin Mary, and also a guild of St Crispin and St Crispian. In addition the 'Friars Minor received 20 bequests from townsmen in the late 14th century and in the 15th, many more than any other religious house'.[31] For example, in a will dated 12 June 1502 Thomas Colfilde requested burial at the Church of St Albright at Stanway, but he also left half a gold angel[32] each to the Colchester Greyfriars and the Colchester Crossed Friars asking both houses to celebrate trentals of masses for the repose of his soul.[33] Of the eight surviving wills dated to this period from the village of Ramsey, some 15 miles from Colchester, two mention bequests to the Colchester Greyfriars. In 1521 Richard Chawles left the Franciscans of Colchester 10 shillings to sing a trental of masses for the repose of his soul.[34] Five years later John Borflete wrote in his will 'I bequeath to the greyfryers of Colchester to pray for me a busshell of whete'.[35]

At the Dissolution the Colchester Greyfriars was surrendered to Richard, Bishop of Dover, who received it on behalf of the king in 1538.[36] Unlike St John's Abbey it presumably surrendered without demur. It is not mentioned in the *Valor*, but in an account for the first year after the Dissolution:[37] Francis Jobson, a farmer, rendered £2 10s 8d for the site of the house, the hall called 'le olde halle', the house called 'le fermerye', the chambers called 'Syr Thomas Tyrrells lodgynge', the kitchen, the bakehouse, the brewhouse, two little gardens and four acres of land. On 8 July 1544 the king granted the premises to him and Elizabeth (his wife), Andrew Dudley, Robert Hennage, Richard Duke and his heirs.[38] The buildings of the convent seem to have largely disappeared shortly afterwards. Although the priory site was not subject to rapid redevelopment, no doubt its building material was in demand.

During its history all the friars and guardians who died at the Colchester convent would have been buried in the priory cemetery. In addition various benefactors also requested burial at the priory. In 1380 Sir John Gernon and his wife, Margaret, were laid to rest on

Reused stones from the Franciscan Priory towards the eastern end of the site.

Reused material from the Franciscan Priory in the neighbourhood of the western precinct wall.

the north side of the choir of the priory church.[39] In 1407 Nicholas Fakenham, who had been elected 28th provincial (head of the entire English province of the order) of the English Franciscans in 1395, died and was buried at the Colchester convent.[40]

Another prominent townsman with links to the priory was John Honyton the younger, son of John and Elizabeth Honyton, a businessman of middle-class west-country origins and a member of a Lancastrian family which had links with the de Veres (earls of Oxford). John's father and namesake had settled in Colchester, and John the younger was involved in the cloth trade with the Low Countries and also had interests in fishing (he owned four ships – or possibly two ships and two half shares in ships).[41] He died in the late autumn of 1485,[42] describing himself in his will as of the parish of St Leonard at the Hythe, and leaving property at the Hythe and outside Rye Gate together with land at West Bergholt. He requested burial at the Franciscan Priory in Colchester.[43] It is interesting that the Colchester Greyfriars remained a desirable place of burial for the laity even at this late date – clear evidence of the respect in which the Franciscan friars were still held. So likewise is the fact that the priory continued to figure significantly in bequests.

Guardians of the Franciscan Priory in Colchester

The guardians of a Franciscan convent did not necessarily hold office for life. Because they came and went rather more rapidly than the heads of other mediaeval religious houses their names are not always recorded, but the following guardians of the Colchester convent are known:

fl. 1419   John Reylegh [44]

fl. 1458–64   Walter Bradenham [45]

fl. 1469   Robert Wotton [46]

fl. 1471   Richard ... [47]

fl. 1475–78	Thomas Lexden [48]
fl. 1482	Robert Howell [49]
fl. 1493	John Tynemouth (or Maynelyn) [50]
1536	John Gurdon [51]

In addition the names of the following Franciscan friars from the Colchester convent are recorded:

1325	Friar Robert Fitzwalter
fl. 1435–47	Friar William Sent [52]
fl. 1435–47	Friar Robert Trumpyngton [53]
fl. 1464	Friar John Horkeslegh [54]
fl. 1466/7	Friar John Bonefaunt [55]
[? *fl.* 1481	Friar Stokes] [56]

Notes

1. The Colchester Blue Badge Guides' *Guide to Many of Colchester's Churches*, Colchester 2001, p. 4, is in error when it states that 'canons were friars rather than monks'.

2. ERO, D/B5 Cr72, m. 19r (transcript, p. 97).

3. *A Guide to Many of Colchester's Churches*, p. 4.

4. C.R. Peers, *St Botolph's Priory, Colchester*, London 1917, p. 12.

5. Peers, *St Botolph's Priory*, p. 12.

6. Peers, *St Botolph's Priory*, p. 10.

7. The dimensions given here for St Botolph's Priory Church are derived in part from *RCHM*, vol. 3, p. 49, and in part from actual measurements taken at the site in January 2008.

8. As marked on the ground today, at 24ft 4in the north-south breadth of the crossing was slightly larger than its east-west length of 24ft.

9. ERO, D/B5 Cr77, m. 6v (transcript, p. 29). The land lay on the south side of *Hethestrete* (modern Hythe Hill).

10. For fuller details see below: St Nicholas's Church.

11. ERO, D/B5 Cr73, m 28v (transcript, p. 138).

12. *Ordo Fratrum Minorum*, or 'Order of Little Brothers'.

13. In the modern Catholic Church there are several orders of friars derived from St Francis's original foundation. There is also a Franciscan order in the modern Anglican Church.

14. However, the modern habit of the Franciscans is more brown than grey. By contrast the Dominican ('Black') Friars wear a black habit and the Carmelite ('White') Friars don a white choir cope on formal occasions.

15. In the orders of friars, the 'provincial' is the elected head of an entire 'province' (usually corresponding to a country).

16. VCH *Essex*, vol. 2, p. 180.

17. *Complete Peerage.*

18. *Frater dominus Robertus Fitzwater, baro fundator conventus Colcestrie intravit ibidem ordinem, Anno Domini milesimo tricentesimo vicesimo quinto*: quoted in Weever (1767 edition) p. 372.

19. J. Weever, *Funeral Monuments*, p. 613.

20. The suggestion by Philip Crummy in *The Colchester Archaeologist*, no. 20 (2007) pp. 24–25, that the church lay further to the north, and that foundations discovered in 2007 may have belonged to it is doubtful for a number of reasons. Crummy believes that the church would have been a cruciform building with transepts and a short east end. This is very unlikely. He also believes that a small square feature shown on an 1847 plan of the site may represent the cloister garth. This seems improbable in view of the feature's size and shape (it measures only 50ft from west to east and is not, in fact, square, but rectangular).

21. Transepts in friars' churches are not unknown but they are rare.

22. 20 December 1463: BL, Add. MS 46349, f. 5v; *HHB*, part 1, p. 158.

23. J. Ridgard, ed., *Mediaeval Framlingham*, Suffolk Record Society, vol. 27 (Woodbridge, 1985), p. 149.

24. The Norwich Blackfriars' slip is only 24ft in width.

25. VCH, *Essex*, vol. 2, p. 180.

26. VCH, *Essex*, vol. 2, p. 180.

27. BL, Add. MS 46349, f. 87r; *HHB*, part 1, p. 304.

28. Catherine had previously bought medicine from John Clerke, a London apothecary (with whom she had settled an account in the sum of 16s. 8d. at the end of March 1464/5). Arundel Castle MS, f. 43v; *HHB*, part 1, pp. 504–05.

29. BL, Add. MS 46349, f. 88v; *HHB*, part 1, p. 309.

30. Part of Kingswood survives as modern Highwoods. For this grant see Pat. 9 Edw. IV, pt 1, m.6.

31. VCH, *Essex*, vol. 9, p. 65.

32. 40d., or 3s. 4d. For mediaeval money, see appendix 1.

33. ERO, D/ACR1 42.

34. ERO D/ACR2 117.

35. ERO D/ACR2 194.

36. *L& P*. Hen. VIII, xiii (2), 1021.

37. Mins. Acts. 30-31 Hen VIII, No. 96.

38. *L& P*. Hen. VII, xix (1), 1035 (73).

39. VCH, *Essex*, vol. 2, p. 180. Their bones might have been among those found in the vegetable garden on the Greyfriars site in the 19th century.

40. *Mon. Franciscana*, i, 538.

41. His will mentions the *Barbara* and the *George* which were 'crayers' (fishing boats?), and also the *Christofer* and the *Valentyn*, together with the latter's nets and equipment.

42. It is possible, though not certain, that he had taken part in the Battle of Bosworth and had been wounded.

43. TNA, PROB 11/7, ff.138v-139r. It is dated 8 October 1485 and was proved on 10 December 1485.

44. VCH, *Essex*, vol. 2, p. 181.

45. VCH, *Essex*, vol. 2, p. 181. Still in office on 16 July 1464. ERO D/B5 Cr72, m. 28r (transcript, p. 139).

46. VCH, *Essex*, vol. 2, p. 181.

47. ERO D/B5 Cr74, m. 28r (transcript, p. 96). 11 July 1471.

48. 1475 – VCH, *Essex*, vol. 2, p. 181. Still in office in 1478: ERO D/B5 Cr77, m. 21v (transcript, p. 112).

49. Not previously attested, but named in ERO D/B5 Cr79, m. 33v (transcript, p. 132).

50. VCH, *Essex*, vol. 2, p. 181.

51. VCH, *Essex*, vol. 2, p. 181.

52. Will of Richard Beche, dated 8 May 1435, proved 10 July 1447. ERO D/B5 Cr61, m. 19v.

53. Will of Richard Beche, dated 8 May 1435, proved 10 July 1447. ERO D/B5 Cr61, m. 19v.

54. ERO D/B5 Cr72, m. 28r (transcript, p. 139).

55. ERO D/B5 Cr73, m. 28v (transcript, p. 138).

56. Soc. Ant. MS 76, f. 37r; *HHB*, part 2, p. 36. Friar Stokes is not explicitly connected with the Colchester Priory.

THE HOSPITALS

In addition to the two priories of St Botolph's and the Greyfriars, late mediaeval Colchester also boasted a third priory, the Holy Cross. This is generally known as Crossed Friars, Crouched Friars or Crutched Friars. Its vanished buildings stood on the southern side of Crouch Street, just to the west of the junction with Maldon Road.[1] We might perhaps have considered this religious house amongst the priories in our previous chapter. However, it was only a priory for the last 40 years or so of its existence. The institution was originally founded as the Hospital of the Holy Cross, and for the greater part of its life it was a hospital rather than a priory.[2] In addition its buildings were not typical of the structures normally associated with a priory. For both these reasons it seems more appropriate to discuss it separately.

A mediaeval hospital bore little resemblance to its modern namesake. It was a religious institution which cared for the poor and infirm within specified categories. Colchester's Hospital of St Mary Magdalen, for example, was established to care for lepers (see p.81). It is not known for whom precisely the Hospital of the Holy Cross was originally founded, but since (like the Hospital of St Mary Magdalen) it stood outside the town walls in what was then still open countryside, it too may have been intended for the care of sick persons who were regarded as contagious. However, an investigation of its affairs in the early 14th century speaks only of the support and relief of 'poor needy men'. From its endowment such a hospital was intended to provide housing, together with care for both body and soul, usually for a defined number of the needy. During the Middle Ages care of the soul was regarded as being at least as important as care of the body.

The Hospital of the Holy Cross seems to have been founded late in the 12th or early in the 13th century. The founder was certainly a lord of the manor of Stanway, and may perhaps have been William de Launvalei who granted the hospital pannage for 12 pigs in his wood at Shrub End in an early but undated charter. The hospital seems never to have been very extensively endowed and was probably always rather poor. Since no foundation charter for this institution survives, we must employ a certain amount of informed guesswork in describing its organisation, but it was certainly in the charge of a master who will have been a priest and who was probably assisted by a small number of brothers. Since the endowment was small, it seems to have been the case that at this hospital, as at others, successive masters gradually reduced the number of serving brothers until the latter disappeared entirely, leaving the entire endowment in the hands of the master alone. It seems doubtful whether the institution was really functioning as a hospital any longer by 1400 and the hospital buildings and chapel were by then certainly in disrepair.

In 1407 King Henry IV took matters in hand. By his establishment, the Guild of St Helen (which was already associated with St Helen's Chapel in Maidenburgh Street) took over responsibility for the Hospital and Chapel of the Holy Cross. The guild undertook to maintain five chantry priests at the hospital and to support 13 poor men there. The choice of the Guild of St Helen was certainly practical. It was a wealthy organisation, named in honour of St Helen to reflect her fabled associations with Colchester as the supposed daughter of 'Old King Cole'. However, St Helen had reputedly rediscovered the True Cross on which Christ was crucified and her name was intimately linked with the cult of the cross.[3] Her guild was therefore well-suited to take charge of a church dedicated to the Holy Cross.

The old hospital foundation continued to exist and, in accordance with the terms of the original foundation, a master or warden of the hospital continued to be appointed. From about 1407 onwards the buildings of the hospital and its chapel were put in order, presumably at the expense of the Guild of St Helen. On the basis of recent excavations, the church or chapel was a small, cruciform building with a central tower but no side aisles.[4] It was probably about 35m in length from east to west,[5] and measured 23m from the north wall of the north transept to the south wall of the south transept. One of the guild members added a new chapel dedicated to the Blessed Virgin on the north side of the sanctuary with its entrance via an archway constructed in the eastern wall of the north transept. This lady chapel was about seven metres in length from east to west and four metres in width, and it housed a newly founded chantry.

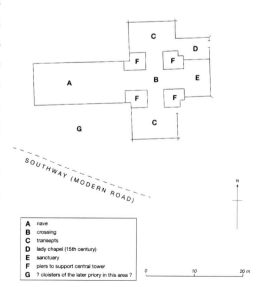

Plan of the Church of the Hospital (later Priory) of the Holy Cross.

A nave
B crossing
C transepts
D lady chapel (15th century)
E sanctuary
F piers to support central tower
G ? cloisters of the later priory in this area ?

It is clear from contemporary records that the church or chapel of the Holy Cross was also now functioning as a parish church (with the warden, presumably, as rector). In 1473–74 the Colchester court rolls record that 'Thomas Meotham, clerk and John, *rector* of the Church of Holy Cross commonly frequent the tavern at the house of Agnes Poitevyn, widow, by night, suspiciously'. Each of the two men was fined 12 pence.[6] Three years later Richard Grene was fined for selling meat in the parish church of Holy Cross instead of in Colchester market.[7] There are further subsequent references in the court rolls to 'the parish church of the Holy Cross'.[8]

The situation changed again in the 1490s when the Crossed Friars regular of the order of St Augustine put forward a claim that the hospital had originally belonged to them and that they had been expelled from it. Although, like the Augustinian canons at St Botolph's Priory, the Augustinian friars followed the rule of St Augustine, they belonged to an entirely separate order.

Not a shred of evidence now seems to survive to support the friars' contention that they had originally held this hospital, and, indeed, it is doubtful whether any real evidence ever existed, since the historic truth of the friars' claim seems very questionable. Nevertheless the friars produced papal bulls and other documents favouring their cause. As a result, in 1496 the master and brethren of the Guild of St Helen, together with Edward Knevit, esquire (lord of the manor of Stanway and hereditary founder of the house), conceded the foundation to the order. At that very late stage, therefore, the old

Reconstruction of the Church of the Hospital (later Priory) of the Holy Cross.

hospital finally became a priory of the Crossed Friars. On the basis of a further papal grant, the prior subsequently sought to claim privileges of sanctuary for his convent equal to those of St John's Abbey. However, the basis for this claim was entirely spurious and since no royal (as opposed to papal) grant of sanctuary rights could be produced, the extravagant claim was not allowed.[9]

The new priory was never rich but it does seem to have attracted some bequests in its limited lifetime. We have already noted two of these. In 1502 Thomas Colfilde, while requesting burial at the Church of St Albright, Stanway, left half a gold angel to both the Colchester Greyfriars and to the Crossed Friars for trentals to be celebrated for the repose of his soul.[10] Richard Chawles of Ramsey also left bequests to both Colchester convents of friars.[11] The short-lived priory of the Holy Cross was dissolved by Henry VIII in 1538 and its property was granted by the crown to Sir Thomas Audley in 1542. At the time of the Dissolution its income was valued at £7 7s. 8d. a year. Portions of the domestic buildings of the priory survived until the time of the Civil War, but in the 18th century (by which time the site was occupied by a workhouse) all the pre-Reformation structures seem to have been demolished.

In the later Middle Ages a cross stood in Maldon Lane (modern Maldon Road) not far from the Church of the Holy Cross. The existence of this cross was recorded in 1470–71.[12] Although stone wayside crosses were not unusual at this period, in this particular instance there seems to have been a direct link between the roadside cross and the nearby hospital dedicated in honour of the Holy Cross. The Maldon Road cross and the other mediaeval wayside crosses of Colchester are discussed in greater detail later (see chapter 5).

Colchester's second mediaeval hospital was that of St Mary Magdalen. Like St John's Abbey, the Hospital of St Mary Magdalen was reputedly founded by Eudo Dapifer at the behest of King Henry I.[13] It was established originally as a hospital for lepers and was therefore sited well outside the town walls, at the junction of Brook Street and Magdalen Street. It is difficult to imagine nowadays, as the traffic roars around the corner at this busy junction, but in the Middle Ages this was open countryside. From the quiet hospital grounds on the hilltop the little Lose Brook from which Brook Street gets its name could be seen flowing prettily in its valley below, crossing the fields of St Botolph's Priory and making its way north-eastwards to meet the northern end of Brook Street before flowing into the River Colne, just beyond East Bridge.

The hospital was in the charge of the abbot of St John's, its upkeep being funded by a grant of £6 per annum from the profits of the manor of Brightlingsea. However, the hospital also had its own master who was *ex officio* rector of the Church of St Mary Magdalen. By the grant of King Richard I the lepers of this hospital were allowed to hold an annual fair on the vigil and feast day of St Mary Magdalen (21 and 22 July).

The authority given to the abbey produced disputes. Early in the 14th century the brethren of the hospital complained to Parliament that, although Henry I had granted to them tithes of the abbey in bread, ale and other victuals for their maintenance, a former abbot, Adam, had persuaded them to show him their charter which he then threw into the fire, and since then he and his successors had detained the tithes. The present abbot, moreover, had detained the £6 rent from Brightlingsea; he had also come in great force to the hospital, demanded their charters and common seal and ordered them to obey him. However, the master Simon de Ia Neylonde and one William de Langham would not carry out his will so he ordered them to be dragged out of their church and to be thrown out and kept out of their house, all contrary to the charters of the kings. When any inquisition was taken on the matter, the abbot was successful on every point and disproved the allegations.[14]

When Henry VIII had all the church property in his realm valued in preparation for the dissolution of the religious houses, the Hospital of St Mary Magdalen was found to be worth just over £11 a year. 'The said hospitall is and hath ben reputed and taken for a parishe church without remembraunce of any man nowe lyving and ther is in the parishe about 4 score husselyng people'. Although the leper foundation was dissolved and the hospital's landed property was granted by Elizabeth I to Nicasius Yetsweirt and William Tunstall, an enquiry undertaken in 1582 restored some property to the master (rector) so that the hospital continued to enjoy a vague kind of existence until the reign of James I. Finding both the foundation and the church in a state of advanced decay, James I refounded the hospital in 1610 as 'The college or hospital of King James.'

Under the terms of this re-foundation there was to be a master (who would also be the rector of the parish of St Mary Magdalen) and five paupers, each of whom were to be given 52 shillings a year from the foundation. The master was to have the nomination of the paupers when vacancies arose, and all the possessions of the old foundation were confirmed. From this point on, the successive masters of the hospital treated the yearly payment of 52s. each to the poor as a fixed sum and considered the remainder of the hospital's income as their own money, a position which was tested and approved in the courts in 1833.

During the 17th century the mediaeval church ceased to function as a place of worship and was for a time used as a poorhouse. By the beginning of the 18th

The mediaeval Church of St Mary Magdalen in 1774.

century it was in ruins, but was brought back into regular use for worship in 1721 at which time the building was repaired by the Lord Chancellor at his own expense.[15] This church building had reportedly consisted at one time of a nave (without aisles) and a chancel with a chapel for the lepers adjoining. However, two engravings dating from 1777 and 1801 both show a small and very simple building which appears to measure only 25ft (or just over 7.5m) in length from west to east. This can hardly represent the entire structure of the original church and it seems likely that by the 18th century only the former chancel of the mediaeval church remained standing and that this alone is depicted in the engravings. In support of this contention one might note that the structure depicted in the engravings is very similar in size to the chancel of the Church of the Hospital of the Holy Cross, which was revealed by recent excavations to measure about 7m from its eastern wall to the central crossing. It may therefore be the case that the Church of St Mary Magdalen as originally constructed was similar in

The mediaeval Church of St Mary Magdalen in 1801.

– 83 –

South side of the 19th-century Church of St Mary Magdalen.

form and size to the Church of the Holy Cross. If so, it too may once have been a cruciform, aisle-less building with transepts and a central tower.

The western wall of the church as illustrated in the 18th century contains a large archway with a window, which has simple mullions and no tracery. This west window appears to be a post-mediaeval insertion and it is possible that the archway in which it was inserted was originally the chancel arch. No traces of ruined structures survive west of this wall in either of the engravings, but there is part of a wall containing an archway, with a statue niche above to the south-west of the church. Its precise location is difficult to interpret but it may represent the south wall of a vanished south transept. Alternatively it could be the only surviving trace of a vanished chapel (possibly the former lepers' chapel).

The west end of the church as shown in the engravings is surmounted by a low bell tower of timber and is flanked by two tall but undecorated hexagonal pinacles. There is a doorway of perhaps 13th-century date placed centrally in the south wall and a blocked window of probably the same date to the west of this entrance. A smaller and later window, perpendicular in appearance and apparently still functional, existed towards the eastern end of the south wall. No depictions survive of the east or north walls but the single-storey buildings of the hospital can be glimpsed behind a low wooden paling to the north of the church.

In the 19th century all the buildings of the hospital (including the church which had

again become dilapidated) were demolished and re-erected. The new church was a small, cruciform building of knapped flint construction. By the second half of the 20th century this new church had become redundant, and it was demolished in 1994 (part of its

Remains of the east end of the Church of St Mary Magdalen.

eastern wall still stands towards the southern end of Brook Street) to make way for the present Magdalen House, which represents the modern incarnation of the Hospital of St Mary Magdalen. Photographs exist of both the interior and the exterior of the 19th-century church.

Incomplete list of the Masters or Wardens of the Hospital of St Mary Magdalen prior to James I's refoundation.

Elias.

Simon de Ia Neylonde.

Roger de Creppyngg, elected 1301.

John Cherche (Prior of the Hospital of St Mary Magdalen), *fl.* 1446–47. [16]

Thomas Gale 1548–57.

Benjamin Clare 1562.

Thomas Lowe 1586.

Notes

1. Crouch Street derives its name from the Crossed (or Crutched) Friars but the later house on the north side of Crouch Street called 'Crutched Friars' does not represent the site of the priory.

2. In a recent account published in the *Colchester Archaeologist* (no. 20, 2007, pp. 19–23) Stephen Benfield assumed the opposite, but actually there seems to be no evidence that the foundation was a priory earlier than the late 15th century.

3. See, for example, VCH, *Essex*, vol. 9, p. 20.

4. S. Benfield, 'The lost church of the Crossed Friars', *The Colchester Archaeologist*, no. 20 (2007), pp. 19–23.

5. The west end was not found in the 2007 excavation of the site since it lay beneath an adjoining building.

6. ERO, D/B5 Cr75, m. 19r (transcript, p. 103).

7. ERO, D/B5 Cr76, m. 21r (transcript, p. 119).

8. ERO, D/B5 Cr79, m. 1v (transcript, p. 4).

9. VCH, *Essex*, vol. 2, p. 181.

10. ERO, D/ACR1 42. A trental comprised 30 masses.

11 ERO, D/ACR2 117. His bequest to the crossed Friars was 12d.

12. ERO, D/B5 Cr 74, m. 14r (transcript, p. 56).

13. VCH, *Essex*, vol. 2, p. 184, citing a charter of Henry II.

14. VCH, *Essex*, vol. 2, p. 184.

15. VCH, *Essex*, vol. 9, p. 327.

16. ERO D/B5 Cr61, m. 8r.

CHURCHES, CROSSES AND CHANTRIES

In addition to its various religious houses, mediaeval Colchester naturally had a number of parish churches and in addition possessed chantries and wayside crosses. Most of the parish churches and one chantry chapel survive, though they have undergone many alterations. We have already encountered four of the parish churches, since the churches of St Botolph, St Mary Magdalen and the Holy Cross all served parishes as well as religious communities, while St John's Abbey operated the Church of St Giles within its barbican as a parish church. Of the other mediaeval religious buildings within the town walls St Helen's chapel, though not in the Middle Ages parochial in its function, still stands, albeit much repaired externally and refurbished within. This former chantry chapel now serves Colchester's Orthodox Christian community.

The mediaeval parish churches within the walls were eight in number: St James the Great, All Saints, St Nicholas, St Runwald, Holy Trinity, St Martin, St Peter and Our Lady-at-the-Wall. In all but two cases a church building still stands, although only two of these buildings now fulfil their original purpose. Two churches unquestionably qualify as lost landmarks: St Nicholas and St Runwald, and these will be fully explored in this chapter.

Our Lady-at-the-Wall and St Peter have both been greatly altered. Nothing further will be said here about the mediaeval appearance of the Church of Our Lady (but see p. 101 'Chantries'). The mediaeval Church of St Peter is treated as a lost landmark for reasons that will become apparent. The remaining four churches, despite the fact that all have been altered, must be passed over with only a very brief mention.

Of these four the Church of St James the Great, although it felt the hands of the Victorian restorers to some extent, still presents a generally mediaeval appearance and functions as a parish church. All Saints and Holy Trinity remain *in situ* but have been more heavily Victorianised and also secularised. Happily the Church of St Martin has fared better. Although redundant as a church, it is now among the best-preserved of Colchester's mediaeval landmarks.

St Peter's Church

The inclusion of St Peter's Church in this book may at first sight seem somewhat surprising since this church still stands to this day on its ancient site at the top of

A 15th-century priest in mass vestments from the Colchester area (Great Bromley).

North Hill on the northern side of the High Street. In what sense then, can St Peter's be considered a lost mediaeval landmark? The fact is that the present day church so little resembles its mediaeval forebear that the latter can indeed be considered lost.

It is probable that there was an Anglo-Saxon church on this site, and the church is mentioned by name in the *Domesday Book* (1086). In fact it is the only Colchester church to be mentioned in the Domesday survey. The dedication of St Peter's Church may have originally been to St Peter and St Paul, for the will of John Thursteyn of Myland, written in 1428 and proved in 1447, refers to this church under that double dedication.[1]

By the 14th century St Peter's was a cruciform church with a central tower. In the 15th century side aisles were added, subsuming the transepts so that the building began to assume a ground plan more closely resembling that of the present church. The exterior of the church was extensively reconstructed in the 18th and 19th centuries. Its central tower, damaged in an earthquake in 1692, was demolished during the 18th century. A new tower was then built at the west end of the church: an innovation which greatly altered the appearance of the building. As for the interior, that was also substantially altered at about the same time by the construction of side galleries. The present, rather dark and gloomy, interior of St Peter's does little to recall the brilliance of its vanished mediaeval glories: the painted and gilded rood screen; the side chapels with their brightly coloured altars; the twinkle of the votive lights; the images of the saints.

The mediaeval *sanctus* bell from St Peter's Church.

Surviving piscina in the south aisle of St Peter's Church.

In the 13th century St Peter's had a Guild of St John the Baptist, to which John Thursteyn of Myland left two shillings. Half a century later, in 1501 there was a cross in the churchyard on the north side of the church, for John Abbot writing his will in that year had asked to be buried next to it.[2] This stone cross was presumably the one from which the gospel was read during the Palm Sunday procession. No sign of it now remains. John Abbot also mentions in his will the Guild of St Barbara in St Peter's Church, and also St Barbara's altar. It would be interesting to know where this stood, as there are no mediaeval side chapels or altars remaining in the church today. However, a piscina survives in the vicinity of what would once have been the south transept. A piscina is a basin, built into the wall, where the celebrant priest could ceremonially wash his hands before the consecration of the bread and wine at Mass. The existence of a piscina always indicates that an altar once stood nearby, even if no other trace of that altar now survives.

John Abbot also left the sum of 10 gold angels for painting and gilding the rood loft in St Peter's Church.[3] A rood loft was a substantial construction, usually of timber, which spanned the chancel arch, surmounting the rood screen which formally separated the chancel from the nave. The rood loft carried the great rood, or crucifix, which constituted the focal point of almost all late mediaeval churches. This loft was used when the priest ascended to offer incense before the great rood, and also for other liturgical functions including singing and the proclamation of the gospel. No trace of the mediaeval rood loft now survives at St Peter's.

In 1501 there was also a 'great stone' on the south side of the church. This was possibly a milestone adjacent to what is now the High Street, giving the distance to London. This stone is mentioned in the will of Robert Fraunces.[4] Robert also refers to

The mediaeval-style reredos from St Nicholas's Church, now in the north aisle of St Peter's Church.

the celebration of a Jesus mass at St Peter's and indicates the existence of a Jesus Guild, for he left money for the master of this guild to buy parchment for recording the names of brethren-donors. Writing his will in the summer of 1502, John Thurske[5] asked to be buried in St Peter's churchyard, near the west end of the church. John Grene,[6] who made his will some two weeks later, left a shilling to the mass of Our Lady and St John at St Peter's Church.

The south gate of St Peter's Church in Corn Hill (the High Street). The mediaeval 'great stone' stood in this area.

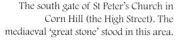

St Runwald's cemetery.

St Runwald's Church

The unusual dedication of this church suggests Anglo-Saxon origins. St Runwald was a grandson of King Penda of Mercia.[7] At the same time, however, the odd location of this church – on an island in the middle of the High Street and market place – together with the fact that its graveyard, which survives, was separate from the building and located in West Stockwell Street, suggest that the church was erected at a date when this central area of Colchester was already fairly built-up. St Runwald's seems unlikely, therefore, to have been an early Anglo-Saxon foundation. It has also been suggested that it may have started life as a chapel-of-ease, only later acquiring parochial status and burial rights.

St Runwald's seems to have been a poor parish, and mediaeval rectors tended not to

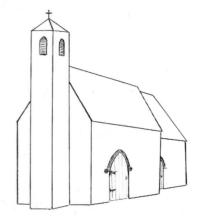

St Runwald's Church as it may have appeared in the 15th century, before the west tower collapsed.

Fifteenth-century arcade from St Runwald's Church, as rebuilt at Stanway.

stay for very long. The church which survived until the 19th century was apparently built in the late 11th or early 12th century with a small rectangular nave and a square chancel, both constructed of coursed flint rubble. Its original appearance was probably not dissimilar to that of the surviving chapel of St Helen in Maidenburgh Street, albeit with the addition of a small chancel. By the late 14th century a western tower had been added.

The shops of Middle Row adjoined the east end of the church, so that when in the 15th century the decision was made to add a small lady chapel, it had to stand on the north side of the chancel to which it was connected by an arcade of two bays. This arcade still exists, having been subsequently re-erected in the Church of St Albright, Stanway.[8] In the later Middle Ages St Runwald's Church housed a guild of St John the Baptist.

By the end of the 16th century the fabric of the church was in a poor state. Judging from the *Prospect of Colchester* of 1669, in the course of the following century the mediaeval tower at the west end may briefly have acquired a small cupola-like roof of square section. By the end of the 17th century, however, the western tower had been entirely demolished and was replaced by a bell turret. In the course of the 18th

The tower of St Runwald's in 1669. The mediaeval appearance has apparently been altered by raising the height slightly and adding a square cupola.

century restorations to the church were carried out in brick and were of a classicising nature. A pediment was added over the south door and round-headed windows were inserted in the east and west walls. By the 19th century, unfortunately, the church was again in a poor state. Moreover, it was deemed to be a nuisance because of its location in the middle of the High Street. It was demolished in 1878 and its parish united with that of St Nicholas's, whose church was enlarged in order to accommodate the parishioners of St Runwald's before the latter was demolished.

In addition to the 15th-century arcade from the lady chapel which survives at Stanway, material from St Runwald's Church was also reused to build the Cloisters Hotel and St Runwald's House in Maldon Road.[9]

St Nicholas's Church

Like other churches in the town centre (Holy Trinity, St Runwald's) the Church of St Nicholas was probably a late Anglo-Saxon foundation dating from the 10th century.[10] The building, which was in part founded upon a pre-existing Roman secular structure, stood on the south side of the High Street facing the northern arm of the L-shaped market place. The church experienced many vicissitudes before its final and regrettable demolition in the mid-20th century. Its site is now occupied by St Nicholas House. Part of the former graveyard – though now in a dismally sad and shabby condition – is still preserved behind the church site to the south. Nineteenth-century

The site of St Runwald's Church today. The tree marks roughly the position of the northern wall.

The 19th-century St Nicholas's Church from the south.

photographs show this area as a delightful oasis of greenery, and since its splendid trees have managed to survive, it seems a great pity that something cannot be done to improve the present grim and tatty state of this little plot.

In the 14th century the Anglo-Saxon Church of St Nicholas was rebuilt in brick and flint. The new church was a cruciform structure, 66ft (20m) in length from east to west with transepts and a central tower.[11] This tower was not square in section but rectangular, measuring 14.27ft (4.27m) from east to west and 15ft 6in (4.72m) from north to south.[12] Somewhat unusually the tower was very nearly centrally located since the chancel to the east of the tower measured 25ft (7.6m) in length, while the nave to the west was 27ft (8.2m) long. Those parts of

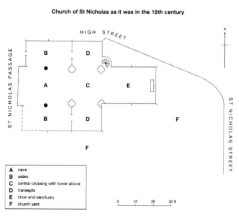

Church of St Nicholas as it was in the 15th century

HIGH STREET

ST NICHOLAS PASSAGE

ST NICHOLAS STREET

A nave
B aisles
C central crossing with tower above
D transepts
E choir and sanctuary
F church yard

0   10   20   30 ft

Plan of St Nicholas's Church at the beginning of the 15th century before the south aisle and transept were rebuilt.

the 14th-century cruciform church which survived until 1955 included the north and west arches of the central crossing (which originally supported the church tower), the west wall of the nave and the east and north walls of both the chancel and the north transept. All of these were considered to be early 14th century in date.

Originally the nave was aisle-less, but within a century of its construction aisles were added subsuming the transepts and depriving the church of its cruciform appearance externally. The north aisle, and the arcade of two bays which divided it from the nave, both survived until 1955 and these were also dated to the 14th century. In the spandrel above the column, separating the two bays of the arcade, there was a round quatrefoil opening which was likewise of 14th-century date.

Although no measurements exist for the 14th-century south transept, the north transept measured 11ft 6in (3.5m) from the north wall to the central crossing and it is probable that originally the south transept was identical in size. When the aisles were added the north aisle corresponded in width to the north-south length of the north transept, and it is highly likely that the south aisle did likewise. In the 15th century, however, this first south aisle was demolished and rebuilt on a much grander scale with its width increased to 20ft (6.1m).[13] At the same time the south transept was demolished and the aisle was extended eastwards to match the combined length

of the nave and chancel. It is not known who was responsible for this considerable increase in size, but in the second half of the 15th century this church was one of those that enjoyed the patronage of Sir John Howard, later Lord Howard and Duke of Norfolk.[14] The new south aisle had a low roof and five large perpendicular windows along the southern side. The two western windows lit up the nave aisle, the central window the area of the former south transept and the two eastern windows the new chapel on the south side of the chancel.

The 14th-century nave of
St Nicholas's Church.

By the 15th century the interior of the church certainly contained tombs, for when he made his will in about 1446 John Clerke asked to buried inside the Church of St Nicholas and close to the tomb of his father.[15] John also left the sum of two gold angels to the church, together with an embroidered red cloth, a green silk cloth and a silver bowl. By 1437 at the latest there was an image of the church's patron, St Nicholas, in the chancel. In his will dated to that year Thomas Fraunceys left money for a wax candle to burn before this statue.

It is possible that by this time a rood and rood screen had been installed in the easternmost bay of the nave. By all accounts there was a conspicuous cross of some kind since Thomas Fraunceys also left funds to maintain a perpetual votive light burning before it. By 1501 there were also images of the Blessed Virgin Mary and of St Antony. Both are mentioned in the will of John Mayston,[16] who asked to be buried in the churchyard and requested his wife to provide great wax candles to burn before these two images. Robert Otewey,[17] who wrote his will just a few months later, also requested burial in St Nicholas's churchyard and left five groats in order that a trentall of masses be celebrated in the church for the repose of his soul. In the 15th century there was a guild named in honour of the still relatively recent cult of Corpus Christi at St Nicholas's Church.[18]

The Reformation undoubtedly changed the appearance of the church interior. From the outside, however, the form and dimensions of St Nicholas's remained more or less unaltered until the end of the 17th century when the central tower collapsed, wrecking the roof of both nave and chancel. By the 1720s the western end of the nave and the south aisle had been repaired and re-roofed, and a small new sanctuary had been constructed between the north-west and south-west piers of the fallen tower. Above the north transept a new low tower was constructed of timber.

The central tower of the mediaeval St Nicholas's Church in 1669, about 50 years before its collapse.

'James', the 15th-century *sanctus* bell from St Nicholas's Church, now at the church of St Martin of Tours, Basildon.

'John', the great 15th-century bell from St Nicholas's Church, also now at the church of St Martin of Tours, Basildon.

The rest of the church was left standing in ruins.

St Nicholas's Church remained in this curious state for more than a century. Then in 1875–76 it was grandiosely reconstructed in Gothic revival style according to the plans of Sir George Gilbert Scott.[19] It is in this last incarnation that St Nicholas's is still remembered by some older Colcestrians. The new Victorian church was a splendid edifice, though it bore only a limited resemblance to its mediaeval predecessor. However, it retained the ancient north aisle and transept, together with the nave and chancel of the old church in reconstructed form. The old north aisle now became a parish room and the north transept continued to be the base of the church tower as it had been since the early 18th century. The simple timber top of the tower was now reconstructed in stone with a tall lead spire, which became a celebrated Colchester landmark (recalling, albeit unconsciously, the vanished spire of the Franciscan Priory Church which had once stood a little further east along the High Street). The old nave and chancel now became the new north aisle, to the south of which a large new nave and chancel were constructed on the site of the 15th-century south aisle.

The new landmark tower of St Nicholas housed the church bells, two of which dated from the 15th century. These were probably originally the passing bell and the *sanctus* bell of the old mediaeval church. The curious English custom of 'change ringing' is a relatively modern (post-Reformation) invention. In the Middle Ages church bells were strictly practical artefacts which were rung for quite specific purposes. A bell was rung at Mass to signal the consecration of the bread and wine. This was the *sanctus* bell, so-called because it sounded first just after the singing of the liturgical chant called the *Sanctus*. In the 15th century when the custom of ringing a signal for the short prayer known as the *Angelus* early in the morning, noon and in the evening spread to England from the Continent, the *sanctus* bell would also be used for that purpose. In addition, a bell was tolled at funerals and solemn *requiems* to signal to the wider community that a soul had passed from this world and to invite prayers for the deceased. One bell could fulfill all these functions if necessary but better-endowed churches would have had two bells and this was clearly the case at St Nicholas.

Of St Nicholas's two 15th-century bells, one is a great bell called 'John', 40in in diameter and cast by Joanna Hille in 1441.[20] The other is a smaller bell called 'James', 31in in diameter and cast by Richard Hille (Joanna's husband) at a date not precisely recorded between 1423 and 1440.[21] The larger bell bears the rhyming couplet *In Multis Annis Resonet Campana Iohannis;*[22] a wish which certainly seems to have been fulfilled. The smaller bell is simply inscribed *Sancte Iacobe Ora Pro Nobis.*[23] Remarkably both bells somehow managed to survive the collapse of the mediaeval church tower in the 18th century.

Although they were also to survive the eventual destruction of St Nicholas it is a great tragedy that, having rung out from Colchester's High Street for 500 years, the sound of 'John' and 'James' is now no longer to be heard there. These 15th-century bells were among the last

The bellfounder's mark of the Hilles on 'John'.

A stone from St Nicholas's Church, now in the Castle Park.

surviving echoes of the authentic sound of mediaeval Colchester. Although they can now be heard (together with the later bells from St Nicholas) ringing out from the modern bell tower of St Martin of Tours' Church in Basildon where they are much loved and cherished, their removal from their original home town represented a significant loss of part of Colchester's mediaeval heritage.

By the mid-20th century St Nicholas's Church was regarded as superfluous and in 1955 was demolished. Its destruction was protested by the townspeople at the time, and has subsequently been widely regretted. However, not all of its stonework is lost. Many fragments of its carved masonry remain (albeit totally unsuspected and unrecognised by most visitors) concealed in the rockery of Colchester's Castle Park.

Which of these ravaged fragments are portions of Scott's 19th-century Victorian Gothic revival stonework and which are the authentic remains of the mediaeval Church of St Nicholas it is now difficult to say.

Fittings from St Nicholas's Church also survive in other churches in and around Colchester. The (modern) reredos from the high altar is now in the north aisle of St Peter's Church, while the pulpit and the font were transported to the Church of St Barnabas, Old Heath, just outside Colchester.[24]

The 19th-century north tower of St Nicholas's Church.

Wayside Crosses

Once upon a time England had hundreds of wayside crosses. Some of these were 'preaching crosses' associated with houses of friars; some were memorials; some for use in the church's Holy Week liturgy and some were for pilgrims signalling the route to a shrine.[25] The most grandiose of such crosses were probably those belonging to the series of 'Eleanor Crosses': royal commissions ordered by Edward I to commemorate his first wife, Eleanor of Castile.[26] Most wayside crosses, however, would have been simpler in design.

Colchester had at least four large stone crosses within the walls or in fairly close proximity to the town, all of which have vanished completely. This is not surprising, for very few such mediaeval crosses survived the Reformation anywhere in England (though it seems something of a mystery why the cross, a quintessential symbol of Christianity, should have been targeted by the reformers). However, a few stone crosses do survive, or survived long enough to have been recorded. In yet more cases the base alone is extant, and in some instances a restored cross has later been re-erected on a surviving mediaeval base.

We have already seen that there was a wayside cross in Maldon Lane (Maldon Road), not far from the Hospital and Church (later Priory) of the Holy Cross. This cross certainly seems to have been connected in some way with the Church of the

Holy Cross. By all accounts the land on which it stood was apparently the responsibility of the Guild of St Helen in the 1460s and 1470s,[27] and this guild, as we know, was responsible for the Hospital of the Holy Cross throughout the greater part of the 15th century. Although there is now no way of knowing exactly what any of Colchester's crosses looked like, the Maldon Road cross may perhaps have somewhat resembled the Whitefriars Cross in Hereford.

Whitefriars Cross, Hereford.

The site of the stone cross in the churchyard of St Peter's.

We have also noted the existence of a cross in St Peter's churchyard on the northern side of the church, which was probably used chiefly for the church ceremonies of Holy Week and Easter. There were also at least two other wayside crosses in the vicinity of Colchester which have not yet been mentioned. A third cross was sited at the end of East Street,[28] possibly in the vicinity of the modern mini-roundabout where the Ipswich and Harwich Roads part company. The fourth cross was beside the road leading to the Hythe. 'In 1404 an acre belonging to the community was described as lying in a field towards Hythe opposite the cross which stands in the highway towards Hythe' (CR 35/14r), and there is mention in 1409 of the common field 'opposite le Hethe Cros' (CR 37/3r). In 1423 an assault was reported as having occurred 'at the cross on this side of Hythe' (CR 43/20r).[29]

Chantries

There were also a number of chantry foundations in late mediaeval Colchester.[30] The majority of chantries were founded only for a specific period of time, but there were also several perpetual chantries which survived until Edward VI filched their endowments and suppressed them.

Newark Cross.

A chantry was an endowment to finance the employment of a chantry priest, who would offer mass for the repose of the benefactor's soul and for the souls of others nominated by him or her. The masses offered were not solemn *requiems* but the ordinary masses of the day, which were offered for the souls of those for whom the endowment was established. A chantry was therefore not necessarily a grandiose and intrusive foundation, and the chantry masses could simply be celebrated at the high altar (or one of the subsidiary altars) in the parish church. In some instances, however, special chantry chapels were endowed by more wealthy patrons. In such cases the chantry masses would have been celebrated in the chantry chapel itself.[31]

The wealthiest and best known of the mediaeval Colchester chantries was undoubtedly that founded by Joseph Elianore, a Colchester burgess of the early 14th century, who served eight times as a bailiff between 1311 and 1342.[32] Joseph, who was also known as 'Joseph of Colchester', endowed St Botolph's Priory with land at Greestead and Ardleigh in 1337. His chantry was established at the Church of Our Lady-at-the-Wall. Provision for the endowment was made in 1338, though it came into effect only on Joseph's death in 1348.[33]

The endowment of Joseph's chantry comprised houses, land and rents. At least some of the property was on the western side of North Street (modern North Hill) and now forms part of the site of Colchester's Sixth Form College. The chantry endowment initially paid the salaries of two chantry priests and provided them with a house in Our Lady's churchyard. By 1362, however, only one chantry priest seems to have been maintained.

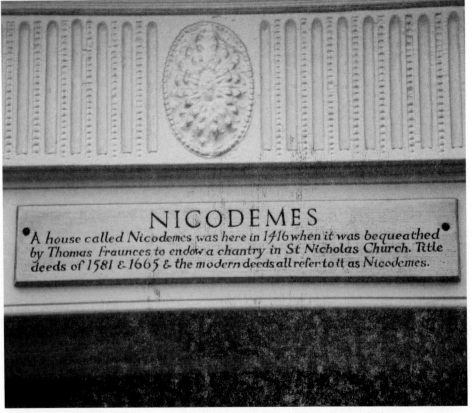

NICODEMES

A house called Nicodemes was here in 1416 when it was bequeathed by Thomas Fraunces to endow a chantry in St Nicholas Church. Title deeds of 1581 & 1665 & the modern deeds all refer to it as Nicodemes.

Plaque in Frere Street (the High Street) relating to the foundation of Thomas Fraunces's chantry.

Joseph Elianore's chantry was established in the chapel of St Thomas the Martyr within the Church of Our Lady-at-the-Wall, and in 1470/1 the court rolls record a debt of £40 owed to William Ketill, clerk, and others relating to repairs to the chantry (meaning presumably to St Thomas's chapel).[34] There are also numerous surviving late-mediaeval records referring to the property which comprised the chantry endowment.[35]

Other notable Colchester chantries were those founded by John of Colchester and Richolda Cofford at St Helen's Chapel in the 14th century, and by John Bayn and Thomas Fraunces at St Nicholas's Church in 1383 and 1416 respectively. A plaque towards the eastern end of the High Street (former Frere Street) between the Minories and the Tourist Office recalls the fact that the property called *Nicodemes* formed part of the endowment of Thomas Fraunces's chantry.

Notes

1. ERO, D/B5 Cr61, m. 7r.

2. ERO, 30CR1.

3. See appendix 1.

4. ERO, 32CR1.

5. ERO, 44CR1.

6. ERO, 41CR1.

7. C. Cockerill and D. Woodward, *Colchester Churches a brief history and description*, Colchester 1973, p. 11.

8. VCH, *Essex*, vol. 9, p. 334 states that the lady chapel at St Runwald's had three bays, but re-erected at Stanway its arcade has only two bays.

9. Cockerill and Woodward, *Colchester Churches*, p. 12.

10. VCH, *Essex*, vol. 9, p. 328.

11. The substantial piers which had supported this tower survived until 1874.

12. This and all other measurements given here for St Nicholas's (unless otherwise noted) are taken from *RCHM*, vol. 3 (*North East Essex*), 1922, p. 40. They are measurements taken while the building was still standing.

13. This measurement is derived from a plan drawn in 1874 before the southern part of the church was rebuilt by Scott.

14. Howard maintained a votive light burning at St Nicholas's Church (Society of Antiquaries of London, MS 76, f. 108v: A. Crawford, ed., *The Household Books of John Howard, Duke of Norfolk, 1462–1471, 1481–1483*, Stroud 1992, pt 2, pp. 149–50). No reference survives in the extant Howard household accounts relating to the rebuilding of St Nicholas, but neither is there any mention of similar work at Stoke-by-Nayland church, despite the fact that the latter was certainly partly rebuilt by John Howard.

15. ERO, D/B5 Cr61 m. 6r.

16. ERO, 19CR1.

17. ERO, 6CR1.

18. VCH, *Essex*, vol. 9, p. 65. The Corpus Christi cult, which reverences the sacramental presence of Christ in the consecrated Host, was instituted by Pope Urban IV's bull, *Transiturus*, in 1264. It was proclaimed a universal feast of the western church by Pope Clement V in 1311 and was celebrated in England from 1318 onwards.

19. This work was in connection with the demolition of St Runwald's and the unification of the two parishes (see above).

20. The first bell known to have been cast by a woman.

21. These two bells (together with all the other bells from the Victorian St Nicholas) are now at the Church of St Martin of Tours, Basildon. For more information see the St Martin's Church website: www.stmartinsbasildon.co.uk/Bell%20Tower.htm

22. 'May the bell 'John' ring for many years'.

23. 'St James, pray for us'. The mottoes of the bells are given in RCHM, vol. 3, p. 40.

24. Cockerill and Woodward, *Colchester Churches*, p. 13.

25. For a survey of such crosses, see A. Rimmer, *Ancient Stone Crosses of England*, London 1875, reprinted 1973.

26. The surviving Eleanor Crosses are at Northampton, Geddington and Waltham Cross. The Eleanor Cross at Charing Cross in London is a Victorian reproduction.

27. ERO, D/B5 Cr73, m. 27r (transcript, pp. 128-29); Cr 74, m. 14r (transcript, p. 56).

28. ERO, D/B5 Cr74, m. 14r (transcript, p. 53).

29. Britnell, *Colchester in the Fifteenth Century*, citing the Colchester court rolls.

30. VCH, *Essex*, vol. 9, p. 65.

31. See C. Burgess, 'A service for the dead: the form and function of the anniversary in late mediaeval Bristol', in S.T. Blake and A. Saville, eds., *Transactions of the Bristol and Gloucestershire Archaeological Society for 1987*, vol. 105, pp.183-211.

32. VCH, *Essex*, vol. 9, p. 58.

33. VCH, *Essex*, vol. 9, p. 324, citing the patent rolls.

34. ERO, D/B5 Cr74, m. 2v (transcript, p. 16). William Ketill was the rector of the Church of Our Lady-at-the-Wall from 1468 to 1476.

35. E.g. ERO, D/B5 Cr75, m. 10r (transcript, p. 58); Cr 77, m. 25r (transcript, p. 131).

CIVIC AND COMMERCIAL STRUCTURES

The Walls and the Castle

In the past Colchester had been a walled town, and the centre of the modern town is still, in part, surrounded by walls which are popularly referred to as 'Roman'. They are, of course, Roman in origin but a glance at the surviving fabric in Priory Street, opposite the ruins of St Botolph's Priory, will suffice to show that as they now stand, the walls contain significant elements of mediaeval rebuilding. In this area new mediaeval bastions were constructed, for the town walls were still important defences and as such they were no doubt regularly maintained and updated at that time.

As for Colchester Castle, that too has Roman foundations but these were originally created to support a temple in honour of the Emperor Claudius. It was not until after the Norman Conquest that they were reused to support a fortification. The precise date of the castle's construction is not recorded but it seems to have been standing by

the reign of Henry I as he granted it to Eudo, founder of the monastery of St John (see chapter two).[1] The castle itself can hardly be considered a lost landmark of mediaeval Colchester since the nucleus of its fabric still stands. However, a brief mention may be justified here since it once had subsidiary buildings which have now vanished, and the castle walls, while probably never as high as those depicted in some reconstructions of the building, have certainly lost their battlements.

A mediaeval bastion in More Street (Priory Street).

Colchester Castle in the mid-17th century viewed from the south. The battlements still appear to be intact. The large, square, south-western tower was later partly demolished then restored with a round, domed turret, beside which a small tree now grows.

In the Norman period and into the 12th and 13th centuries, the castle, like the town walls, was considered an important defensive structure. By the later Middle Ages, however, although the castle still rejoiced in a royally-appointed constable, the building itself was seen as of little practical use and its upkeep was neglected. It still served as a gaol, but in the 15th century there were reports of prisoners escaping. This was blandly attributed by officials to the fact that the roof was collapsing. Thus, on 20 May 1455 the patent rolls recorded the grant of a pardon to John Hampton Esquire, then Constable of Colchester Castle, for having allowed prisoners to escape, 'on his shewing that the gaol within the castle is of such age and weakness that the roof fell by night and so the ...prisoners escaped.'[2] A second pardon was issued to Hampton under identical circumstances on 2 December 1461.[3] By this time royalty on visits to Colchester no longer bothered to call at the dilapidated castle, preferring to stay in the greater comfort and safety of St John's Abbey.

The town walls were likewise sadly neglected by the 15th century. From a defensive point of view they had become largely redundant and, except as a possible source of building materials, were probably generally seen as an irrelevance. There is no evidence from the surviving records that the walls were being maintained at this period while prosecutions in the court rolls indicate that, in spite of fines, their fabric was regularly being plundered. In 1470/1 members of the prominent Christmas family and others found themselves in court for digging out sand from under the town walls near Our Lady's Church.[4] Later the same year a tiler called John Strut was fined for having sold six cartloads of stone from the town walls to a Frenchman.[5] During the same period John Merveyn was accused of destroying the walls 'with dung and water flowing from his tenement',[6] while William Oldehalle was fined sixpence for reputedly constructing the foundations (*le pynnyng*) of his new houses at Head Gate using stone from the adjacent town walls.[7] For a single year this number of prosecutions indicates that the town walls were subject to significant attack by the town's inhabitants. The fact that this part of England has little in the way of naturally occurring stone suitable for building acted both as an incentive to plunder the walls and a disincentive to the borough authorities to repair them.

Since fairly extensive sections of the town walls still survive along Balkerne Hill, in Vineyard Street, in Priory Street, along the former eastern perimeter of the Greyfriars property and running through the Castle Park, they, like the castle, are dubious candidates for inclusion in a survey of lost landmarks and for this reason

A similar view of Colchester Castle today.

they will not be explored here in great detail. However, some mention is justified by the fact that certain sections of the walls are entirely lost, or (as at Claudius Court) do not extend much above ground level. Moreover, all but two of the town gates which were in use in the mediaeval period have vanished[8] and a brief commentary on the town walls forms a useful introduction to a review of the lost mediaeval town gates of Colchester.

Gates

Roman Colchester seems to have started life with five principal town gates.[9] Balkerne Gate in the centre of the western wall and East Gate in the centre of the eastern wall stood at either end of the *decumanus maximus* (or main east/west street), while North Gate and Head Gate stood at either end of the *cardo maximus* (main north/south street). At the eastern end of the south wall a further large gate, South Gate (or St Botolph's Gate) allowed egress in the direction of the hippodrome. The Roman names for these gates are unknown and those used here are the mediaeval and modern names.

Balkerne Gate fell into disuse at a very early period and its role as the main exit from Colchester in the direction of London was taken over by Head Gate. In the mediaeval period Balkerne Gate was known as King Cole's Castle, and mediaeval Colcestrians may not have realised that this structure had ever been a functioning gateway. The other four principal Roman gateways remained in use throughout the mediaeval period and the sites of all of them are known, though all four of these gates have disappeared. Ironically, the formerly redundant Balkerne Gate survives in part and has returned to use as a means of

Plaque marking the site of Head Gate.

The site of Head Gate.

entry to and egress from the area within the old town walls.

The precise appearance of Colchester's principal mediaeval gates is uncertain, though recent excavations on the site of Head Gate indicated that, in the Roman period at least, this entrance had a central pier and consisted of two archways standing side by side. Head Gate may have retained this structure into the mediaeval period and might therefore have somewhat resembled the vanished East Gate of Chester, which was demolished in the 18th century but of which engravings survive.

The site of East Gate.

Plaque marking the site of East Gate.

However, Colchester's East Gate is depicted in a view of the town dating from the 1580s as a single archway with a crenellated wall above and standing between two substantial bastions which appear to have been square or rectangular in section. Similar mediaeval gateways which survive elsewhere, both in England and abroad, often have one or more upper storeys. Colchester's East Gate may likewise have possessed at least one upper storey, though the surviving depiction does not appear to suggest that either the central block or the flanking bastions rose significantly higher than the adjoining town walls.

The mediaeval North Gate has been depicted and described by Patrick Denney as a three-storey, timber-framed structure, crowned by a row of three pitched and tiled roofs.[10] The gateway described and illustrated by Denney undoubtedly existed and appears to have resembled a grander version of the surviving Schere Gate. The actual entrance to the town comprised a single rectangular opening with no archway of any kind. There can be little doubt that the North Gate looked like this in 1724 when it was depicted on Pryor's Prospect of Colchester. Although by the end of the 18th century the main part of the gatehouse spanning the carriage way was gone, one part of the side structure of the building survived until the 1850s and photographs of it remain.

However, we must be wary of accepting Denney's description of this 18th-century structure and its 19th-century survivals as 'mediaeval'. The Colchester court rolls show clearly that during the second half of the 15th century the town's North Gate was in a semi-ruinous condition. In the 1480s the mediaeval structure finally collapsed and for some time its fallen ruins lay blocking the road.[11] Thus, the North Gate which Denney depicts and describes dates only from around the 1490s. Since Henry VII ascended the throne in 1485, this makes the three-storey, timber-framed gatehouse of which we have pictures Tudor rather than mediaeval. It therefore remains open to question whether the mediaeval North Gate was a

Schere Gate in the early 20th century.

timber-framed or a stone-and-brick building, and whether it possessed one or more archways or had a simple rectangular opening like its Tudor successor.

No depictions appear to survive of Colchester's South Gate and it is not known whether it had double arches like Head Gate, or whether the carriage way at those entrances was spanned by a single arch as at East Gate and (perhaps) North Gate.

In addition to the main gates, several smaller gateways also pierced Colchester's town walls. Some of these may have dated from the Roman period, but others, like Schere Gate, seem to have been mediaeval structures. The name 'Schere' is derived from the mediaeval English word *sherd* meaning a small gap. Schere Gate, a pedestrian entrance in the centre of the southern town wall, is mentioned in the mediaeval records under that name.[12] It provided egress from the town in the direction of St John's Abbey and gave access to Colchester's licensed brothels so it probably saw a good deal of traffic. Despite the disappearance of both abbey and brothels Schere Gate survives and remains in use today.

The long-vanished Rye Gate was the corresponding gate in the middle of the northern wall. It gave access to Middle Mill and the countryside beyond. The broken line between Schere Gate (via Trinity Street) and Rye Gate (via Maidenburgh Street) marked the north/south division between the mediaeval wards of Colchester.[13]

At least two small postern gates also existed during the Middle Ages. One opened onto *More Strete* (modern Priory Street). No trace of a mediaeval gate is now to be seen in this area, so this postern was presumably located in a section of the wall where little of the mediaeval fabric now survives. In fact, there is a later doorway with steps in Priory Street in a section of the wall which has been rebuilt in brick, not far from the private road leading to J. Watts. This could well be on the site of the mediaeval More Street

The postern gate in More Street (Priory Street) as it is today.

postern, the private road being perhaps the old *More Elm Lane*. A second postern gate in the western wall just south of the Church of Our Lady-at-the-Wall features very frequently in mediaeval records. Like Schere Gate, this is still in use today – although only just ('improvements' to Balkerne Hill in the second half of the 20th century having rendered pedestrian activity in the vicinity somewhat hazardous).[14]

In mediaeval times the maintenance of the town gates was the responsibility of the town's two annually-appointed chamberlains, and it is evident from the 15th-century records that, rather like modern politicians, these wily officials cared less for the state of the gates than for the purses and the good opinions of those who might have to foot the bills. Evidently they saw repairing the gates as a potentially costly and probably useless undertaking. As a result, the chamberlains were repeatedly cited before the borough courts for failing to keep the town gates in good repair.

No doubt at one time the town's stone and brick gateways actually had reinforced wooden gates or doors which could be opened and closed. However, it is clear that by the second half of the 15th century these wooden structures had disintegrated. Evidence that the rot had set in came in 1470/1 when it was reported that South Gate was in a ruinous condition.[15] In the same year the chamberlains were cited for failing to put up chains at East Gate and a post and chains at Head Gate. The reference to chains is very interesting as it reveals that there were no longer any actual gates in place. Instead (presumably as an economy measure) provision had been made for chains to be strung across the open gateways to form a token barrier. This was a matter for concern as by law the town gates were all supposed to be closed at night to stop movement in and out. Some means of obstructing entry and exit was therefore essential.

By 1473/4 the chamberlains were under attack again. This time it was stated that Head Gate was in a ruinous and dilapidated condition.[16] Given that Head Gate was the main entrance and exit to and from Colchester in the direction of London it is abundantly clear that the town gates were no longer regarded as of any real importance and were not even a matter of civic pride. However, it seems that the experiment with chains had now been abandoned in favour of something a little more substantial. In the same year the chamberlains were also cited for their failure to maintain locks, keys and iron bars at East Gate, and in 'the ports', or postern gates of More Street (modern Priory Street) and Magdalen Street.[17] Although the provision for iron bars and locks initially appears to suggest that the matter of the gates was now being taken more seriously, what emerges is that once again nothing had actually been done. The accusation was repeated almost word for word later the same year.[18] Moreover, the surrounding stone and brick structures of the gateways were also being neglected. The North Gate was repeatedly reported to be in a dangerous condition, and this point was finally proved dramatically when the persistent neglect finally caused the structure to fall down in the 1480s.[19]

The Moot Hall

The chamberlains, who so significantly failed to maintain Colchester's gates in the later Middle Ages, had their office at the moot hall on the site of the present town hall. Its existence was first recorded in 1277 but it was actually even older, since Colchester had been granted the right to have its own justices in the 12th century and parts of the building demolished in 1843 certainly dated from that period.

The old moot hall was a stone building, some 40ft (12m) in length from east to west with a hall on the first floor.[20] An engraving of this building survives showing it as it stood in 1824. There were entrances on the north and south sides. The southern doorway – which comprised a stone archway, eight or nine feet (2.5m) in maximum height and about the same in width, with double doors of panelled

The Moot Hall.

timberwork probably of oak construction – opened onto the High Street. The northern entrance gave out on to a large courtyard and garden which also housed some of the market stalls. Both doorways had steps which were replaced on the initiative of the bailiff William Reyne in 1373/4. Reyne gave the north door tiled stone steps and the main south door marble steps. The south door was flanked by two large mullioned windows. One of these survived until the demolition of 1843 and its carving has been linked with the workshop which made the west doorway of Rochester Cathedral in about 1160. By the 16th century there was a bell turret rising above the roof over the south door but it is not known when this was constructed.

The moot hall served as the meeting place for the town council and also as Colchester's law courts. In addition, it housed the office of the town clerk. The building also had other functions. Steps from the courtyard led down to a whitewashed cellar which was leased out as the town's wool market. The same steps also led to the town gaol where prisoners could be confined, although alternatively they were sometimes chained up outside the entrance to the moot hall instead. This practice had two main advantages: the prisoners could beg for food from the passers-by and they were visible to the populace thereby serving as a warning. Colchester's pillory also stood in front of the moot hall.

The Pillory and Gallows

Pillories were designed for the punishment of offenders, who were usually confined by having their arms and neck locked between two wooden beams. They were then exposed to the insults and ridicule of passers-by. There is mention of the existence of such a structure in Colchester in the Court Rolls for 1463–64[21], and John Barbour was in 'Le Pillory' in 1470/1,[22] but in neither instance is the location of the device specified. However, it is known that at a later date Colchester had a pillory in what is now the High Street opposite the moot hall, which survived until at least 1807.[23] It is probable that the location of the pillory had remained unchanged over the centuries.

Colchester also claimed the right to its own gallows in 1274.[24] There is reference to *Galwystrete* (or *Galwestrete*) in the 1470s in connection with John Auncell, who was a farmer at Mile End (or Myland – even today, both spellings of this place name continue to be used).[25] Some have interpreted this road name as 'Hallows Street' but 'Gallows' seems more likely. However, the exact locations of both the street and the gallows remain unknown. It is probable, though, that the gallows stood outside the town and on a main road (where its use could provide both a warning and an example to passers-by). Since mediaeval Mile End seems to have been focused some distance to the east of the area which now bears that name and closer to the Ipswich Road (in the vicinity where Myland farm still stands), it may be that the gallows was located beside the Ipswich Road, not far from the modern Tesco's/St John's roundabout.

The Market Place

Colchester must have had a market from a very early period, but the earliest surviving reference is in 1189 when a charter specified that the markets should remain as confirmed by the justices in eyre in the reign of Henry II. In 1285 it was said that Wednesday and Saturday were the market days, but in the later Middle Ages it was claimed that the common market was held every day, and since there are extant records of market sales on Monday, Tuesday, Wednesday, Thursday, Saturday and Sunday during the 14th and 15th centuries this claim appears to have been true.

Although Colchester's market is reported to have been spread through the town (rather as it is today) the main area in which it was held was L-shaped, with the upright stroke of the 'L' comprising the High Street from St Nicholas's Church to the junction with North Street (North Hill) and Headgate Street (Head Street). The horizontal stroke at the bottom of the 'L' was formed by an open space off the High Street, just opposite St Nicholas's Church and bounded on the eastern side by what is now the top (south) of Maidenburgh Street; on the western side by George Street; and to the north by the eastern end of William's Walk. This block of land has subsequently been filled in with buildings but its slightly odd shape suggests that it may once have been an open space, and records of 11 January 1478/79 relating to property deals by Richard and Matilda Maidstone provide evidence that the mediaeval market place did indeed extend north of the High Street into this area.[26]

The relevant records relate to two properties which the Maidstones were selling: a rentar near what was then the top of the eastern side of Maidenburgh Street (and backing onto the land of Colchester Castle) and a messuage facing the rentar on the opposite side of the road. Detailed descriptions of the locations of these two properties are provided and from this information we know that on the southern side of the messuage (and therefore on the west side of Maidenburgh Street) there was a little lane which gave access to the market place. This lane must have opened into what is now William's Walk.

There was some attempt to allocate market space in an ordered fashion between the various kinds of merchandise on offer. In general terms the shambles (butchers' stalls) were near the Moot Hall and the east end of St Runwald's Church. However, the butchers' stalls may also have extended further east into the space notionally occupied by the cloth merchants and leather workers, for there are reports of butchers throwing offal into the castle ditch. The stalls for the tanners and butchers were fairly solid and permanent structures built of timber. The butter market was opposite the Moot Hall. Fish was sold on the south side of the High Street, probably roughly opposite St Runwald's Church. Grain was marketed at the western end of the High Street which was then known as Corn Hill, while in the Middle Ages the vegetable market was in the area stretching to the north of St Nicholas's Church. These locations were not completely static and there are records of changes being made at later periods.

Colchester's market must often have been as notable for its stench as for its sights. In 1447 John Grene, John Cay, Seman Whytefoot, Alice Fyshwyf, Margaret Barker, Anne Risby and Margaret Smyth were all fined for dumping fish entrails in the market place.[27] Later, in 1470/1 John Baley, Richard Ball, Thomas Baroun, Robert Cok, Thomas Their, John Aldham, Henry Piggesle, Peter Barkere, John Fouler and Thomas Corbet, all of whom were butchers, found themselves in trouble for throwing offal in the gardens of East Stockwell Street.[28]

The household accounts of Sir John, Lord Howard (later Duke of Norfolk) give us some idea of the range of foodstuff which could be purchased in Colchester's market in the second half of the 15th century. These accounts show that damsons were sold, together with sugar, sugar candy, spices (including pepper, cinnamon and saffron), almonds, nuts, raisins, figs and vinegar.[29] However, supplies of spices and figs were also sometimes brought from London for the Howard household, so perhaps the full range of these items (most of which must have been imported) was not always available in Colchester.[30] Given Colchester's proximity to the coast, it is hardly surprising that a good selection of seafood was available, including mussels, oysters and shrimps.[31] Porpoise could also be found there.[32] In 1482 Lord Howard paid 12d. 'to Carters son of Colchester for bryngyng of a qrtr porpays'.[33] The Colchester records reveal that in 1498–99 there was a Colchester fishmonger called John Carter,[34] though whether this John was the lad who had brought Howard the porpoise or the boy's father remains uncertain since the first name of neither father nor son is mentioned in the Howard accounts.

Fish for the Howard household was also purchased at Colchester's Hythe, for example on 19 March 1483 when 'my Lord bought [fish] at the Hythe, of a man of the coast'.[35] Purchasing fish at the Hythe is only what one might expect, but it is perhaps more surprising to discover that the Howard household also obtained bread there. On Michaelmas Eve 22 September 1482, 'my Lady paid to the baker at the Hythe upon reckoning, for bread for [the] household 8s.' The fact that she was settling a bill indicates that this was not a one-off purchase and only a week later on 28 September 'my Lady paid to the baker at the Hythe in full payment of bread comen into the household unto the said day 11s.'[36] In the 1480s the Hythe probably consisted just of a couple of rows of small houses, a bridge (first licensed in 1406/7 but rebuilt in 1473) and two watermills – for grinding grain and for fulling cloth.[37] The mills at the Hythe presumably account for the presence of the baker favoured by Margaret Chedworth the second Lady Howard. A mill is shown on the earliest surviving map illustrating the Hythe[38] and there is specific mention of 'the mellar of Colchestre, at the Hethe' in Howard's accounts for April 1467.[39]

Mills

Although later maps and engravings of Colchester illustrate windmills (one of which seems to have been constructed on top of a ruined tower of the castle) in the Middle Ages, the main and most obvious source of power for driving mills in the Colchester area was not the wind but the water of the River Colne and its tributaries. Water-driven mills were used both for grinding grain into flour (grist mills) and for finishing cloth (fulling mills). There was avid competition between the various mills. For example 'in 1429 St John's Abbey complained that Colchester burgesses had set up roadblocks to prevent men grinding corn or fulling cloth at the abbey's mills.'[40]

The cloth industry was very important to Colchester's mediaeval economy and must have constituted a strong incentive to construct fulling mills, or to convert existing grist mills to serve a dual purpose. Fulling is the process of beating the cloth in a tub of water containing either urine or a special kind of clay called 'fuller's earth', in order to clean and thicken it. After fulling, the wet fabric was suspended to dry on frames called *tenters* by means of *tenterhooks*. Since cloth making was such a significant industry in mediaeval Colchester, not only fulling mills but also tenters must have been a familiar sight around the town. The tenters would have been set up on open ground outside the town walls and along the riverbanks.

A Colchester watermill in use for fulling, 1777.

Watermills can be constructed with either vertically or horizontally-mounted waterwheels. However, in England mills with vertical waterwheels constituted the usual type and we may presume that Colchester's mediaeval watermills were generally of this design. Watermills can be constructed in a stream or river, but the more usual procedure is to divert some of the water along a narrow channel to make it rotate a turbine or waterwheel. The wheel is fitted with paddles so that the force of the water compels it to revolve which in turn rotates an axle driving the machinery of the mill.

Not far from Colchester, and just north of the village of Lexden, stood Lexden Mill. Middle Mill stood on the section of river bank closest to the town walls just outside Rye Gate. East Mill stood next to East Bridge, and belonged to St Botolph's

Middle Mill in the early 20th century before the building was demolished.

MIDDLE MILL COLCHESTER

Priory from at least 1311 until the Dissolution. A former mill building (though dating from a much later period) is still extant on this site and was recently converted into flats. There was a mill at the Hythe known as the Mill in the Wood. There are references to Hythe Mill which may or may not have been the same structure. To the south east of the town, on a tributary of the Colne, stood Cannock [Canwick] Mill and Bourne Mill, which belonged to the canons of St Botolph's Priory and the monks of St John's Abbey respectively. The name Cannock – originally 'Canon's Wick' – still recalls the mediaeval connection with the Augustinian canons of St Botolph's.

Bourne Mill, as it now survives, is a 16th-century stone building standing beside a dammed millpond and incorporating reused stone from St John's Abbey. However, this mill's existence can be documented back as far as the 12th century. The

The abbot of Glastonbury's fish house at Meare in Somerset may suggest the mediaeval appearance of Colchester's Bourne Mill.

An unidentified Colchester watermill, from an engraving of 1767.

Domesday survey of 1086 had recorded six watermills in the Colchester area including three in Colchester itself, two at Lexden and one at Greenstead, but none of these seems identifiable with Bourne Mill.[41] It is possible that Bourne Mill was built by the Benedictine community of St John's Abbey (and later rebuilt by the Lucas family) to fulfill three functions, for it may have served simultaneously as a grist mill, a fulling mill and a monastic (and later aristocratic) fishing lodge (with the millpond doubling as a fish pond).[42]

In addition there were other mills in the Colchester area which, by the later Middle Ages, seem to have been used only for the fulling of cloth. These were North Mill and New Mill (both of which were in the vicinity of North Bridge and just outside the North Gate) and also Stokes Mill at the end of Land Lane. Then there was Hull Mill below Cannock Mill on the stream to the south of the town. This last mill also belonged to St Botolph's Priory. Hull Mill actually comprised two mills, one of which was for milling grain, while the other was for fulling cloth.[43]

The names of some of Colchester's mediaeval millers are on record. Dr Chris Thornton gives the following list in connection with Bourne Mill:[44]

1326	John Rogger
1333	John atte Halle (later miller at Middle Mill)
1336–40	John Wyger (later miller at North Mill)
1345–46	John Stokfyssh (also miller at North Mill)
1352	Thomas Knop
1353	John Knyght, John Pulham and John Dollard (John Knyght, also miller at Old Mill, seems to have been the actual miller of this consortium)
1356–66	Thomas Knop

1372   John Bellamy

1374–78   John Smart

1406   John Potton

1413–14   Thomas Sawyer

1525   Thomas Buxstone

This list indicates that millers moved around a good deal from one mill to another and that they often held the lease of a particular mill only for a year or two.

In 1446/7 Richard Patoun was the miller at Middle Mill. In the same year Thomas Pyers was the miller at Cannock Mill, John Betele at Hull Mill, John Chapman at the Hythe Mill and John Peverell at Lexden Mill.[45] However, by 1470–71 John Chapman had moved to Middle Mill.[46] Subsequently he must have moved again, for in 1476/7 the miller at Middle Mill was Roger More though Chapman was still alive at the time and working as a miller.[47] Another miller named in the same year was Robert Boner but we are not told where he worked.[48] By 1483/4 the miller at Lexden Mill was Robert Moundford.[49]

Streets

Some of the mediaeval streets of Colchester had what is described in the records as 'pavement'. The University of Michegan's online Mediaeval English Dictionary defines 'pavement' as 'the paved, tiled, or otherwise hardened surface of the ground, a street, the floor of a house, church, sepulchre, etc.'[50] Presumably when it refers to the streets of Colchester this word means that they were cobbled. Confirmation for this interpretation can be found in the prosecution of John Cokk, one of the town's butchers. In 1477–78 Cokk found himself in trouble for taking stones from the pavement at St Botolph's Gate.[51]

In 1470/1, in a curious mixture of languages, the court rolls recorded that Thomas Eyr had broken the pavement in front of his own gate in East Stockwell Street with his two-wheeled cart.[52] Three years later Thomas Martyn was prosecuted for having broken the 'pavement' in Wire Street.[53] In the same year (1477/8) the pavement in East Stockwell Street in front of the houses of John Hyde of Nayland and John Aldam was reported to be ruinous and dilapidated,[54] though it is not clear whether either (or both) of the named residents were considered to be responsible for the damage. It is uncertain whether the street called Clay Street, near North Mill, was paved – possibly not, since it was outside the town walls – but Richard Pecok found himself in trouble for digging up this street to extract some of the clay from which it derived its name.[55] John Thursteyn (who was a potter and thus presumably in need of clay) was guilty of a similar offence in 1484/5.[56]

Bridges

In the Middle Ages, as is still the case today, Colchester had two principal bridges: East Bridge and North Bridge. 'North Bridge, recorded in 1189, stood on the site of a Roman bridge or ford, as presumably did East Bridge, recorded from 1238.'[57] These two main bridges were maintained by the borough authorities, as was the ominously named Falling Bridge which seems long since to have finally collapsed definitively, but which once led towards Mile End and was therefore probably located somewhere between the other two.

In general, other bridges were maintained by the parishes within which they were sited, though some small bridges seem to have been the personal responsibility of a single landowner. Thus the bridge which was in need of repair in 1484/5 in the parish of St Michael, Myland,[58] seems to have been the responsibility of that parish. However, William Heynes, whom we met earlier in connection with his failure to keep up the river banks on Brownsford River,[59] was evidently also charged with the maintenance of a bridge over that river known as *Raneynbregge*. We know this because he failed in that duty as well.[60] In the case of *Raneynbregge* we have a possible hint of evolution and progress at work, for the name of the river – 'Brown's ford' – appears to suggest that in the not too distant past this waterway had possessed no bridge and had to be forded.

There is one reference in relation to Colchester which speaks of masons being employed to build a bridge in the late 14th century. However, despite this, and the fact that the bridge at the Hythe was known as *le stonebregge*,[61] every other surviving record indicates that both North and East Bridges were of mainly timber construction throughout the Middle Ages, as indeed they remained until the end of the 16th century and probably longer. It is possible that the masons had been required to build a stone pier or two in the river to help to support a mainly timber construction. Not until the 18th century is North Bridge known to have been reconstructed in brick (later replaced with cast iron). East Bridge was reconstructed in brick in the early 19th century (though it too was later widened and improved with the use of iron).

Colchester's bridges seem to have been poorly maintained in the later Middle Ages. In 1463/4 the chamberlains were censured because North Bridge was ruinous and dilapidated, and later in the same year East Bridge, North Bridge and Falling

Bridge were all reported to be ruinous.[62] Whether anything was done about this is not known, but three years later North Bridge was again said to be ruinous.[63] This particular circumstance may perhaps have been connected with the activities of William Mann (presumably the same William Mann who was sexton of St Nicholas's Church), for in another court record we learn that in 1466–67 'with his two-wheeled cart [Mann] broke the bridge called *le Northbregge*'.[64]

Even if the damage to North Bridge in 1466–67 was solely due to William Mann's carelessness with his cart, it is clear that the repairs (if any) which had been carried out in 1463/4 did not last very long. In 1477–78 East Bridge was again reported to be ruinous and dilapidated,[65] and the chamberlains were also called to account for the fact that both North Bridge and a bridge called *Franchisbregge*, which led in the direction of Nayland, were in a ruinous condition.[66] This report appears to suggest that the borough authorities were also responsible for *Franchisbregge*, though that structure is not listed elsewhere as being maintained by the borough. The chamberlains were again in trouble over the condition of East Bridge in 1483–84,[67] and overall one can only conclude that either the bridges received very little attention or that they were subject to a very great deal of wear and tear.

The bridges maintained by the borough were not the only ones which caused problems. In 1463–64 Sir Thomas Cobham damaged Park Bridge,[68] and in 1473–74 Thomas Wynter, a clerk, was in trouble for having demolished the bridge in Homefeld.[69] Homefeld lay in the south-eastern suburbs to the south of the highway leading to the Hythe (modern Magdalen Street and Hythe Hill).[70] Since the River Colne does not flow in that vicinity, the bridge in question must have spanned a small watercourse or brook (though the only record of a watercourse in this area seems to be when one was illicitly diverted to flow down Magdalen Street – see chapter one).

In some mediaeval contexts the use of the word 'bridge' may be slightly misleading, since to modern ears it tends to imply a rather substantial construction. However, small mediaeval footbridges, which may have consisted of little more than a length or two of planking, were no doubt very easily and quickly erected or taken down. In 1466–67 the courts decided that Thomas Sonday was responsible for the construction and maintenance of a bridge in the lane at the end of North Street (modern North Hill) but the structure which they envisaged was probably a very simple one.[71]

On the other hand, when the town bailiffs made indentures with 10 businessmen who lived at the Hythe for a bridge to be constructed over the river there, they seem to have intended it to be a serious and substantial construction. The new bridge was to span 'the said river and water for a way for all maner people thereon to pass as well with hors and cartes as otherwise'. The bridge was to be built of 'stone or tymber or bothe', and must be of sufficient height to allow shipping to pass beneath. Moreover, once they had built it, the businessmen were also required to maintain it.[72]

The Port

The River Colne's closest approach to the town walls of Colchester is just to the west of the millpond at Middle Mill, where the river bank is approximately 100 yards (or metres) from the line of the wall. Indeed, for the entire short stretch from Middle Mill westwards as far as North Bridge, the river flowed within close sight of the walls (when the latter were still standing in that area). However, the river is not deep enough at this point to be navigable by anything larger than a small boat with a very shallow draft.

Colchester may possibly have been a river port in the Roman period, but at that time the main access to and from the walled town was by road. It seems to have been the Anglo Saxons who first developed a river port for Colchester, a mile and three quarters down river, well to the south-east of the town and only about a mile upstream from Wivenhoe. This port became known as the 'Hythe'.

By the middle of the 12th century, by dint of dredging to deepen the river bed, it proved possible to bring commercial vessels a mile further upstream so that ships could then unload their cargoes only three quarters of a mile from the town. The new landing point was named 'New Hythe' and by extension the old landing place became the 'Old Hythe'. The latter was gradually transformed into 'Old Heath' as the real meaning of its original name was forgotten.

The New Hythe had some privately owned facilities such as quays and warehouses. In 1477/8, for example, John Honyton's private quay at the New Hythe was described as ruinous.[73] Premises (comprising a house and shop) called *le warehous*, mentioned in 1484/5, were privately owned by William and Margaret Smyth of the Hythe.[74] However, there were also public facilities at the port provided by the borough council which certainly viewed the Hythe as a source of income. 'The publicly owned assets there included several buildings, two cranes, and apparatus for weighing and measuring merchandise.'[75] One of the cranes at the Hythe was mentioned in the Colchester court rolls in 1466/7.[76] All cargoes, whether arriving at the Hythe or being shipped out, were taxed and the tax farmed out by the borough on an annual basis, usually to one of the Hythe residents. A small

The Hythe in the early 20th century.

community established itself at the little port consisting of a mixture of traders, mariners, fishermen and other workmen of various kinds. Some, like the local brewer and the Hythe miller, undertook work which served the community rather than being directly connected with shipping.

Mediaeval shipping arriving at the Hythe may have come directly from the Baltic or from the Aquitaine but far more will have consisted of trans-shipments from London. For example, on 2 September 1482 Lord Howard, a shipowner himself, paid 16 pence 'for havenge doune of a tonn [of] wyne in to the shippe, owt of my Lordes seler in London', and he paid a further 12 pence to 'younge Lalford for his costes to go be water to Colchester' with it.[77] Presumably this barrel of wine was landed at the Hythe and transported on to its final destination (perhaps Howard's house in Colchester High Street) by cart. Even more of the shipping activity at the Hythe probably involved local fishing vessels.

Access to and from the New Hythe was by means of Colchester's South Gate (St Botolph's Gate) and Magdalen Lane (modern Magdalen Street). Although Magdalen Lane was paved (possibly cobbled) for much of its three-quarter-of-a-mile length, the roadway from Colchester to the Hythe ran mostly through open fields. At one point on its journey it passed the Hythe Cross (see chapter two – Wayside Crosses). At the beginning of the 15th century the town council authorised the construction of a footbridge over the Colne at the Hythe, but at that time this was limited to a single span not exceeding 18in in width. The footbridge was to be of sufficient height to permit boats to pass beneath and was not to be used by horses or carts.[78] Later in the 15th century, as we have already seen, a larger and more substantial structure was authorised by the borough authorities, constructed and maintained by a private consortium.

Notes

1.   S.A. Moore, ed., *Cartularium Monasterii Sancti Iohannis Bapiste de Colcestria*, 2 vols. London 1897. Vol. 1 p. 27.

2.   *CPR 1452-1461*, p. 242.

3.   *CPR 1452-1461*, p. 645.

4.   ERO, D/B5 Cr74, m. 1v (transcript, p. 5).

5.   ERO, D/B5 Cr74, m. 2r (transcript, p. 7).

6.   ERO, D/B5 Cr74, m. 2r (transcript, p. 14).

7.   ERO, D/B5 Cr74, m. 23r (transcript, p. 84).

8. The two gates which were in use in the mediaeval period, and which survive, are Schere Gate and the postern gate by St Mary's (Our Lady's) Church. Balkerne Gate was not in use during the Middle Ages.

9. There was also originally a sixth gate but it seems to have been small and little-used, and was later blocked.

10. P. Denney, *The Changing Face of Colchester* (Derby: Breedon Books 2002), pp. 36–37.

11. J.A. Galloway, *Colchester and its region, 1310–1560. Wealth, Industry and Rural-Urban mobility in a Mediaeval Society*, unpublished PhD thesis, University of Edinburgh, 1986, pp. 63-65, citing the Colchester Court Rolls.

12. For example, in ERO, D/B5 Cr75, m. 17v (transcript, p. 95).

13. The east/west division was along the line of the High Street.

14. For example, in ERO, D/B5 Cr75, m. 2 (transcript, p. 7).

15. ERO, D/B5 Cr74, m. 2r (transcript, p. 11).

16. ERO, D/B5 Cr75, m. 2 (transcript, p. 7).

17. ERO, D/B5 Cr75, m. 2r (transcript, p. 11).

18. ERO, D/B5 Cr75, m. 19v (transcript, p. 107).

19. Galloway, thesis, pp. 63-65, citing the Colchester Court Rolls.

20. This description is based on VCH, *Essex*, vol. 9, p.274, and on R.H. Britnell, *Colchester in the Fifteenth Century – a Portrait* (http://www.dur.ac.uk/r.h.britnell/Portrait%203htm), both of which supply original source references.

21. ERO, D/B5 Cr72, m. 19v (transcript, p. 101).

22. ERO, D/B5 Cr74, m. 14r (transcript, p. 54).

23. VCH, *Essex*, vol. 9, p. 155.

24. VCH, *Essex*, vol. 9, p. 48.

25. ERO, D/B5 Cr74, m. 14r (transcript, pp. 53, 55).

26. ERO, D/B5 Cr 81, m. 20v (transcript, pp. 67-68).

27. ERO, D/B5 Cr61, m. 15r.

28. ERO, D/B5 Cr74, m. 23r (transcript, p. 86).

29. BL, Add. MS 46349, f. 87r, Soc. Ant., MS 76, f. 30v, Soc. Ant., MS 77, f. 47r; *HHB*, part 1, pp. 304-05, part 2, pp. 25–26, pp. 369-70.

30. BL, Add. MS 46349, f. 85r, Soc. Ant., MS 76, f. 28r; *HHB*, part 1, pp. 299-300; part 2, p. 22.

31. BL, Add. MS 46349, f. 87r, Soc. Ant., MS 76, f. 30v, Soc. Ant., MS 77, f. 47r; *HHB*, part 1, pp. 304–05, part 2, pp. 25-26, pp. 369–70.

32. Arundel Castle, MS, f. 45r; *HHB*, part 1, p. 509. This purchase of porpoise mentions no specific location, but occurs in the context of purchases at St Osyth.

33. Soc. Ant., MS 76, f. 145r; *HHB*, part 2, p. 208.

34. B.*OB*, p. 141, and *OB*, f. 113r.

35. Soc. Ant., MS 77, f. 47v; *HHB*, part 2, p. 371. The not inconsiderable cost of 40s. was borne by Howard's

man, Barker and Howard's debt to him was noted in the accounts.

36. Soc. Ant., MS 77, f. 7v; *HHB*, part 2, p. 292.

37. Britnell mentions 'a mill known as the Mill in the Wood, somewhere near [the] Hythe': Britnell R.H., *Colchester in the Fifteenth Century – a Portrait* http://www.dur.ac.uk/r.h.britnell/Portrait%203html.

38. A map showing the siege of 1648: http://www.trytel.com/~tristan/towns/colcmap1.html.

39. BL, Add. MS 46349, f. 136v; *HHB*, part 1, p. 396. There were, however, mills in Colchester itself (Middle Mill and East Mill).

40. C. Thornton, *Bourne Mill, Colchester – Historical Report*, unpublished, 2007, p. 23.

41. Thornton, *Bourne Mill*, p. 19.

42. For a full discussion of these points, see Thornton, *Bourne Mill*, pp. 23, 67–69.

43. VCH, *Essex*, vol. 9, p. 261.

44. Thornton, *Bourne Mill*, p. 20.

45. ERO, D/B5 Cr61, mm. 8r; 15v.

46. ERO, D/B5 Cr74, m. 14r (transcript, p. 56). He may or may not be identical with John Myller who was at Middle Mill in the autumn of 1470: ERO, D/B5 Cr74, m. 2r (transcript, p. 7).

47. ERO, D/B5 Cr76, mm. 2v, 3v (transcript, pp. 8, 18).

48. ERO, D/B5 Cr76, m. 10v (transcript, p. 61).

49. ERO, D/B5 Cr80, m. 10r (transcript, p. 28).

50. http://quod.lib.umich.edu/m/med/lookup.html.

51. ERO, D/B5 Cr77, m. 11v (transcript, p. 56).

52. *Thomas Eyr fregit pavimentum coram le burgate eiusdem Thome cum bige sue.* ERO, D/B5 Cr74, m. 14r (transcript, p. 55). An alternative entry gives Thomas's surname as 'Their': ERO, D/B5 Cr74, m. 2r (transcript, p. 8).

53. ERO, D/B5 Cr75, m. 2r (transcript, p. 10).

54. ERO, D/B5 Cr77, m. 12r (transcript, p. 57).

55. ERO, D/B5 Cr74, m. 14r (transcript, p. 54). I have not succeeded in identifying Clay Street.

56. ERO, D/B5 Cr81, m. 21r (transcript, p. 73).

57. VCH, *Essex*, vol. 9, p. 234.

58. ERO, D/B5 Cr81, m. 21r (transcript, p. 73).

59. See above, chapter 1.

60. ERO, D/B5 Cr74, m. 29r (transcript, p. 99).

61. ERO, D/B5 Cr61, mm. 8v, 15r.

62. ERO, D/B5 Cr72, m. 11v, 19v (transcript, pp. 61, 103).

63. ERO, D/B5 Cr73, m. 18v (transcript, p. 87).

64. ERO, D/B5 Cr73, m. 18v (transcript, p. 88).

65.   ERO, D/B5 Cr77, m. 2r (transcript, p. 6).

66.   ERO, D/B5 Cr77, m. 11v (transcript, p. 55).

67.   ERO, D/B5 Cr80, m. 20r (transcript, p. 68).

68.   ERO, D/B5 Cr72, m. 19v (transcript, p. 102).

69.   ERO, D/B5 Cr75, m. 19v (transcript, p. 107).

70.   ERO, D/B5 Cr78, m. 3r (transcript, p. 16).

71.   ERO, D/B5 Cr73, m. 27r (transcript, p. 130).

72.   ERO, D/B5 Cr75, m. 7r (transcript, pp. 34–36).

73.   ERO, D/B5 Cr77, m. 2r (transcript, p. 7). Honyton had many business interests at the Hythe.

74.   ERO, D/B5 Cr81, m. 24v (transcript, pp. 84/5).

75.   Britnell, *Colchester in the Fifteenth Century*.

76.   ERO, D/B5 Cr73, m. 27r (transcript, p. 131).

77.   Soc. Ant., MS 77, f. 3v; *HHB*, part 2, p. 286. 'Young Lalford' is probably Thomas Lalleford, a member of a Colchester family.

78.   Britnell, *Colchester in the Fifteenth Century*.

DOMESTIC STRUCTURES

Private houses

Ordinary private houses in mediaeval Colchester comprised *tenements* and *rentars*. The former derived their name from the French verb *tenir* (to hold) and were freehold property. Rentars were investment property let by landlords to tenants. Sometimes a good deal of information is available about such properties. For example, in 1481/2 Thomas Balstone of Colchester, a carpenter, and his wife Agnes (who was the widow of John Hancock of Colchester) conveyed to John Dowe, John Shipman, William Beche and Richard Melke a rentar and garden situated on the south side of the road leading to the church of the Holy Cross (Crouch Street). This property, which was to the west of Head Gate, measured 26ft in length along its frontage on Crouch Street and went back from the road 64ft. On its western side it adjoined another rentar which was already held by John Dowe. On its eastern side the property

'Timperleys', an upper-class, 15th-century Colchester town house belonging probably to the Timperley family of Hintlesham, Suffolk (relatives by marriage of John, Lord Howard, Duke of Norfolk and Constable of Colchester Castle).

abutted a tenement which had formerly belonged to John Hancock and which had evidently been left to his wife, since it was now held by Agnes and her second husband Thomas Balstone. This suggests that the rentar which was changing hands (and behind which was a garden also owned by Thomas and Agnes) had previously formed part of John Hancock's estate.[1] The whole block of property mentioned in this transaction may have stood in approximately the area currently occupied by the building of the former Odeon cinema.

Although its dimensions are given we have no actual description of any part of the rentar in Crouch Street. By contrast, while many other references to private property omit measurements, they may instead supply other interesting snippets of information. Thus in 1466, for example, John Martyn had a tenement situated in the town suburbs in East Street, 'beyond East Bridge' and we know that this dwelling had glazed windows.[2] That this point is mentioned specifically may mean that it was a somewhat unusual feature. Nevertheless, a glazier called John Carter is known to have been at work in Colchester at this period.[3]

Some of the property in the town served a commercial purpose. For example, in Frere Street (now the eastern part of the High Street) there were two shops on the northern side next to the stone wall of the Greyfriars convent.[4] These were probably on the site currently occupied by the white building known as 'East Lodge' which,

until recently, housed the Central Clinic. Several members of the Cook (or Cock) family seem to have been butchers, and in 1476/7 William Cook secured a licence to set up a shop in East Street.[5]

There was also provision for the poor and needy who might otherwise have found themselves homeless. We have already seen that the hospital of the Holy Cross seems to have fulfilled this function, but there were also almshouses within the town walls of

Part of a mediaeval shopfront preserved at the end of Trinity Street.

mediaeval Colchester. A plaque on the north side of Eld Lane recalls the former presence of the almshouses known as 'Lady Darcy's' reputedly founded by Mary Darcy, Countess Rivers (died 1644). Indeed the almshouse buildings themselves still survive – albeit in the form of a later rebuilding – and are now converted into shops. However, there were almshouses in Eld Lane long before Lady Darcy's day so it seems that her role in their establishment may have been exaggerated. Most probably she merely refounded them or extended the benefaction in some way. There is a clear reference to the existence of almshouses in *Eldelane* as early as 1481/2.[6]

Although the mediaeval streets of Colchester had names, many of which are the same as (or very close to) the names they bear today (see appendix 3), the individual houses were not numbered. Generally houses were identified by the name of their owner or former owner. Thus, on one single membrane of a court roll we find mention of a tenement at Head Gate, late of Bartholomew Neve, and another in East Stockwell Street, late of John Browning. Other houses may have had their own names (independant of those of their owners). Thus the same membrane refers to a tenement in the parish of St Nicholas called 'Helle'. The property at Lexden known as 'Kyngges' could be either an example of a house name or a possessive form of the

Former almshouses in Eld Lane, now converted into shops.

The Craftsman and the east side of Trinity Street.

owner's surname.[7] The house where John Sadler lived, in Colchester's south ward, was known as *Bardolf hous* in the 1460s.[8] Possibly this and other house names were simply derived from the names of (unrecorded) previous owners.

Only rarely is it possible to identify with any exactitude the modern occupants of specific mediaeval Colchester properties. However, quite a precise record is preserved in the court roll for 1473–74 relating to the eastern side of Trinity Street.[9] From this it is possible to deduce that in the second half of the 15th century the plot which is currently occupied by Colchester's public library (or part of it) probably comprised two gardens, which in 1473 had recently been in the ownership of John Kymberle and Margery Sparwe. At its western end, where it extends to Trinity Street, the modern library building probably also covers some or all of the property (house and garden) of Thomas Bocher.

Between the library and the present-day craftshop called The Craftsman lies the probable site of a gate which gave access to a *grange* belonging to Simon Mate. In mediaeval English *grange* retained the meaning which it still has in French, so Simon Mate's property was a barn of some sort. The Craftsman itself, together with its two southern neighbours, Tindall's art shop and the Christian Science Church, occupy the sites of three 15th-century rentars. The names of their occupants in 1473–74 are not recorded. Possibly the street frontage of The Craftsman represents the original street frontage of all three rentars, and this view is supported by the existence of a painted white property boundary line on the modern pavement. It is possible that the premises of The Craftsman still incorporate parts of the late mediaeval building.

South of the Christian Science Church stands Timbers restaurant, another building which may actually date back to the 15th century. Its street frontage is level with that of The Craftsman which tends to confirm that this represents the original building line for this side of Trinity Street. In the 15th century the site of Timbers restaurant comprised a tenement which had also recently belonged to Simon Mate (though it had actually been occupied by William Mate – presumably a relative of Simon). The present restaurant building may well incorporate Simon Mate's actual tenement. By 1473/4 this tenement had passed into the ownership of John Neuman of Lavenham and his wife, Margaret, who were then to hand it over to John Reynolds, a relative of Margaret's deceased former husband, Robert Reynolds.

Next to Timbers nowadays is the eastern building of the Trinity Centre. This occupies the site of a rentar owned in the 1470s by Simon Mate and let by him to

'Timbers' Restaurant.

Robert Joynour. South of this building the record of 1473/4 unfortunately does not extend, so we cannot identify the 15th-century owners or occupiers of the sites now belonging to Clive Richardson and Associates, Chartered Surveyors and The Purple Dog (formerly 'The Clarence') public house.

There are other instances where the modern location and usage of mediaeval property can be more or less identified. On 10 May 1475 John Boteler senior, a Colchester mercer, and his wife, Alice, agreed to sell two rentars to William Flyngaunt and Thomas Flyngaunt. The houses stood 'in the suburbs of Colchester outside Northsherd [Rye Gate]'.[10] They were just north of the town wall and on the eastern side of the roadway leading from Rye Gate to Middle Mill. This site would now appear to be occupied approximately by the south-western corner of the boating lake in the Lower Castle Park, or by the park gardens just to the west of the lake.

Occasionally the process of urbanisation can be glimpsed in progress. In 1476/7 William and Alianora Gamday sold to Henry Clerk and Thomas Hobelot a piece of land 93ft long and 13ft wide which was clearly in what is now called Middleborough for it is described as lying outside the North Gate, near the stone wall and Balkerne Lane (modern Balkerne Hill). This piece of land was said to contain 'divers houses, newly built'.[11]

Dunghills

One very conspicuous landmark of mediaeval Colchester whose disappearance we may find little cause to regret is the dunghill. It was, of course, against the law to deposit dung in the town (or in the vicinity of the town). However, the frequent prosecutions and fines recorded against those who broke this law prove beyond doubt that dunghills were a real and notable feature of mediaeval Colchester.

Among the most persistent of the dunghills were those which sprang up in East Stockwell Street. An examination of the Colchester court rolls covering just a few years in the second half of the 15th century shows that the East Stockwell Street dunghill was in evidence in 1466/7 and on numerous occasions in 1470/1. It was still there (or it had returned) in 1473/4.[12] Presumably it disappeared, or was at least reduced in size for short periods following prosecutions, but it seems to have quickly re-established itself after a brief interval.

Somewhat surprisingly, another location which frequently harboured a dunghill seems to have been the area in front of the Moot Hall in the High Street.[13] Possibly a dunghill in this area provided a handy source of ammunition for throwing at malefactors unfortunate enough to find themselves clamped in the adjacent pillory (see chapter six – The Pillory and Gallows). Nevertheless the fact that the dairy market (*Les Butterstalles*) was also sited in this vicinity raises some concerns over matters of health and hygiene. The proximity of the seat of the borough authority itself might also have been expected to inspire greater respect but, in fact, it is clear that some of the borough officials were themselves not above contributing to the problem. In 1481/2 the chamberlains were prosecuted, found guilty and fined sixpence for creating a dunghill behind the Moot Hall, 'in the garden corte called *Moothalle Yerd'*.[14] Three years later they were in trouble again for making a dunghill in the adjacent market.[15]

Another dunghill was reported towards the eastern end of the market place opposite the Bell Inn.[16] Colchester had many other problem locations and additional dunghills are reported within the town walls on various sites, including opposite Holy Trinity Church,[17] in the street opposite St Runwald's cemetery,[18] in Culver Lane,[19] in North Street[20] and in St Helen's Lane.[21] They also caused problems outside the town walls: against the walls of St Botolph's Priory, by the postern in Head Ward, by Our Lady's Church, opposite East Mill, near the cross at the end of East Street and at Magdalen Green, among other places.[22] The Hythe, too, had its dunghills. *Fumaria* (as the mediaeval Latin of the court rolls sometimes picturesquely calls them) were even heaped up against the precinct walls of St John's Abbey.[23]

Nor was solid waste matter the only problem. Liquid waste products also caused a nuisance. The slops of Our Lady's Church were thrown over the town wall by the postern gate,[24] while the already unsavoury East Stockwell Street was regularly rendered still more obnoxious by the local butcher Robert Cok, who was in the habit of discharging *les pissepotts* from the windows of his dwelling into the road beneath.[25] However, since urine in the streets of the town centre has again become a problem in recent years, the contents of Robert Cok's *pissepotts* may no longer qualify, strictly speaking, as a *lost* Colchester landmark.

In a period when sanitation was rudimentary, the Colchester dunghills will inevitably have been composed largely of human excrement. However, the mediaeval town air was probably also perfumed by the animals which were kept within the walls. Horses will have been a frequent sight, as will the horse dung which they left behind them. Nor were horses and their dung exclusive features of *mediaeval* Colchester. As recently as the early 20th century both horses and horse dung were to be seen on the town streets.

Domestic animals were meant to be kept under restraint and not allowed to wander about the town. However, prosecutions and fines prove that this law too was broken. Pigs in particular were not infrequently to be seen loose in the streets.[26] Even when domestic animals were enclosed this could present problems. John

Shipman (husband of Margaret) was a weaver[27] and later a servant of John Howard, Duke of Norfolk. In fact he may have fought with Howard at the Battle of Bosworth in 1485. John Shipman lived in Frere Street in the vicinity of the present 'Minories'. In 1470/1 Shipman and his friend Richard Baldwyn were prosecuted for blocking the king's highway (presumably Frere Street) and then using the resulting enclosure for feeding their ducks.[28] There are also several records of prosecutions in respect of straw and slops from a barn in Culver Lane which were polluting the street.[29]

Discarded offal was another mediaeval landmark whose passing needs no lament. The Colchester butchers found themselves in trouble from time to time for discarding the bones, offal and horns of the animals they slaughtered and sold in inappropriate locations, including against the abbey walls, in the castle ditch and on the ground in the market place.[30] In 1447 Roger Brasynhed and Robert Pecock, both butchers, were reported for 'daily throw[ing] entrails in Casteledych'.[31] It is not clear what waste material William Leche was in the habit of depositing in Maidenburgh Street that same year, but whatever it was it had blocked the gutter near Robert Benale's garden and was the cause of complaint.[32] The nearest modern equivalent to all this would presumably be the half-consumed products of fast food purveyors which today tend to litter the town streets.

Notes

1. ERO, D/B5 Cr79, m. 15 (transcript, pp. 58/9).

2. ERO, D/B5 Cr73, m. 14v (transcript, p. 69).

3. ERO, D/B5 Cr73, m. 30v (transcript, p. 149).

4. ERO, D/B5 Cr73, m. 28v (transcript, p. 134).

5. ERO, D/B5 Cr76, m. 10r (transcript, p. 58).

6. ERO, D/B5 Cr79, mm. 17r, 23v (transcript, pp. 67, 94).

7. ERO, D/B5 Cr74, m. 13r (transcript, p. 49).

8. ERO, D/B5 Cr73, m. 22r (transcript, p. 104).

9. ERO, D/B5 Cr75, m. 13v (transcript, p. 76).

10. ERO, D/B5 Cr76, m. 20v (transcript, p. 114).

11. ERO, D/B5 Cr76, m. 30v (transcript, p. 172).

12. ERO, D/B5 Cr73, m. 27r (transcript, p. 129); Cr 74 mm. 2r, 14r, 23r (transcript, pp. 8, 54, 86); Cr75, m. 2r (transcript, p. 7).

13. ERO, D/B5 Cr74, mm. 2r, 14r (transcript, pp. 7, 53, 55/6).

14. ERO, D/B5 Cr79, m. 26r (transcript, p. 106).

15.   ERO, D/B5 Cr81, m. 21r (transcript, p. 73).

16.   ERO, D/B5 Cr72, m. 1v (transcript, p. 7). For details of the Bell Inn, see chapter 8.

17.   ERO, D/B5 Cr73, m. 18v (transcript, p. 87).

18.   ERO, D/B5 Cr74, m. 14r (transcript, p. 54).

19.   ERO, D/B5 Cr75, m. 2r (transcript, pp. 7, 9).

20.   ERO, D/B5 Cr76, m. 2r (transcript, p. 7).

21.   ERO, D/B5 Cr75, m. 2 (transcript, p. 7).

22.   ERO, D/B5 Cr72, m. 11v (transcript, p. 61); Cr74, mm. 14r, 23r (transcript, pp. 53, 86); Cr77, mm. 1v, 18r
      (transcript, pp. 5, 92); Cr80, m. 10r (transcript, p. 26).

23.   ERO, D/B5 Cr79, m. 1v (transcript, p. 5).

24.   ERO, D/B5 Cr72, m. 19v (transcript, p. 100).

25.   ERO, D/B5 Cr81, m. 21r (transcript, p. 74).

26.   ERO, D/B5 Cr 72, m. 19v (transcript, p. 100); Cr74, m. 1v (transcript, p. 4); Cr76, m. 2r (transcript, p. 6).

27.   ERO, D/B5 Cr72, m. 31r (transcript, p. 154).

28.   ERO, D/B5 Cr74, m. 2r (transcript, p. 10).

29.   E.g. ERO, D/B5 Cr74, m. 23r (transcript, p. 83).

30.   ERO, D/B5 Cr 79, m. 15v (transcript, p. 64); Cr 80, m. 10r (transcript, p. 28).

31.   ERO, D/B5 Cr61, m. 8r.

32.   ERO, D/B5 Cr61, m. 8r.

FACILITIES FOR EDUCATION AND ENTERTAINMENT

Music

Mediaeval Colchester was capable of making its own music. We have already encountered the surviving mediaeval bells of the parish churches of St Peter and St Nicholas, together with records of the lost great bell of St Botolph's Priory. By the 15th century probably every Colchester church had at least one bell. Many will have had two, and a few of the largest and most wealthy may recently have acquired a third bell to be used especially for the thrice-daily ringing of the *angelus*.

The church services were frequently accompanied by music, and we know that the priory church of the Greyfriars had organs. It is probable that other Colchester churches also had small mediaeval organs and choirs of singers.

The town was also home to waites and mistrels. Waites were semi-professional musicians who sang popular 'carols' – not only at Christmas but also at other seasons. On Tuesday 21 April 1467 Sir John Howard 'gave the waites of Colchester 16d,'[1] and another year, just after Christmas, Howard's steward 'took to the minstrels of Colchester 20d.' Later, Lord Howard's accounts also refer to the presence of a professional harpist in Colchester. On 28 October 1482 'my Lord made covenant with William Wastell, of London, harper, that he shall have the son of John Colet of Colchester, harper, for a year, to teach him to harp and to sing, for the which teaching my Lord shall give him 13s. 4d. and a gown; whereof my Lord took him in earnest 6s. 8d.'[2]

Inns and Taverns

The town had both inns and taverns. Notionally, the difference between the two seems to have been that inns provided accommodation and possibly stabling, whereas taverns were simply places to drink, but as we shall shortly see the distinction was not so clear-cut in practice. Britnell states that at the beginning of the 15th century 'Colchester had about 13 inns where travellers might stay and between 15 and 20 taverns where townsmen and visitors alike could buy wines imported from Gascony. These amenities were an established part of the town's trading organisation, since merchants met there to negotiate sales and to settle their accounts.'[3]

The sign of the Bull Inn.

In the Howard household accounts we see that while inns rejoiced in names like The Swan or The Bull, taverns may simply have been known by the name of their owner. Before going to St John's Abbey on 27 December 1482 Lord and Lady Howard had been at 'Noles', where Lord Howard had partaken of a 'potell of wine' and some other drink, while his lady had a pint, at a total cost of 1s. 4d.[4] Either 'Nole' or 'Noles' presumably represents the name of a tavern-keeper. Actually no such surname is found in contemporary Colchester records but John *Noke* was certainly a Colchester taverner at that period, so probably 'Noles' is an error or a mistranscription. However, once again the picture is not clear-cut, because if Noke was the man whose establishment the Howards visited in 1482, the reference could well be to The White Hert Inn (see p.145).

The number of drinking establishments seems to have considerably diminished during the course of the 15th century from the numbers quoted by Britnell. In the Colchester court roll for 1446–47[5] only eight men are named as 'taverners'.[6] The eight men in question (with details of their area of residence added where known) are:

John Baroun   South ward
John Crouley
Richard Fitz
John Fleccher

John Hayward	Head ward
John Kebbull	
John Poole	North ward
John Rouge	St Nicholas's parish

John Rouge actually owned two establishments, one of which (presumably the one where he did not himself live) was let to John Fleccher.

This list of so-called 'taverners' raises certain problems. John Kebbull, who is named in 1446/7 as a 'taverner', is known previously to have kept something grander than a mere drinking establishment, for he had been the innkeeper at the Swan Inn.[7] Does this list of 'taverners' then actually represent the innkeepers of Colchester? In support of this idea we may note that nine names of inns are recorded at about this period, one of which seems not to have been in business in 1446/7.[8] The known inns were:

The Angel[9]	North ward	St Runwald (?)
The Bell	South ward (?)	St Nicholas
The Bull[10]	Head ward	Our Lady
The Falcon[11]	North ward	St Peter
The George[12]	North ward (?)	St Nicholas
The Saracen's Head	Head ward	Holy Trinity
The Star	North ward(?)	St Runwald
The Swan[13]	Head ward	(?)
The White Hert[14]	Head ward	St Peter (?)

Of these The Star seems not to have been functioning in 1446–47. The George cannot be proven to have been in existence in 1446–47, but it was in being by the end of the 15th century and architectural features of the building have been dated to c.1450.

It seems likely that John Kebbull was running The Swan in 1446–47, given that he is known to have been its landlord 10 years earlier (when he was fined for depositing dung in the street).[15] As for John Baroun, he lived in South ward and the only inn known to have been in that ward was The Bell. It therefore seems likely that Baroun ran this inn in St Nicholas's parish. John Rouge also has to be accommodated somewhere in the parish of St Nicholas, so it seems likely that if

Baroun ran The Bell, Rouge must have owned and lived at The George. The other associations are more difficult to determine. John Hayward in Head ward could have been landlord of The Bull, The Swan or The White Hert. Since no evidence has so far emerged as to where the other four landlords lived, it is impossible to assign them to their correct inns. It nevertheless seems possible to marry the list of 'taverners' with the contemporary list of Colchester inns, thus suggesting that this list of so-called 'taverners' does, in fact, represent innkeepers.

By 1463–64 The White Hert was owned by John Noke, who was then leasing it to John Skeet. Skeet proved to be an unsatisfactory tenant who failed to maintain the property, as a result of which Noke took him to court.[16] The outcome is unknown but if John Noke took the running of The White Hert back into his own hands it may have been this inn which Lord and Lady Howard visited in 1482. The White Hert was certainly an inn which enjoyed Howard's patronage at about that time. Noke himself had died by the autumn of 1481 but his wife remained in the trade.[17]

We know from his household accounts where Lord Howard stabled his horses when he and his attendants were in Colchester. The Bell, The Bull, The Hert and

The back courtyard of the Bull Inn.

The Swan are all mentioned in this connection. Of these only The Bull in Crouch Street still exists – Colchester's oldest surviving inn. In the 15th century it stood just outside Head Gate on the London road. The present building retains some features dating back to the 15th century, although there have been many alterations. Tithes of three groats were paid to the abbot of St John's in 1461.[18]

The Hert (otherwise The White Hert – the name is derived from the badge of Richard II) stood at the western end of the High Street, just west of the site of the present Bank Passage. The earliest surviving reference to this inn dates from 1437 when the owner William Stanton was fined for depositing dung behind the inn, which may indicate that it already had stables at that date.

The Swan lay just behind The Hert in Helle Lane. Some have tried to identify Helle Lane with modern Culver Street West, but this cannot be correct for there are clear references to 'Culver Lane' in the 15th century, and it opened into Headgate Street (Head Street), therefore making it identical with the modern Culver Street West. Helle Lane was perhaps an adjacent side street in the neighbourhood of the modern Bank Passage. In 1437 The Swan's owner John Kebbull was fined, along with William Stanton, for the same offence of depositing dung, suggesting that this inn too may have had stables at that time. It seems that in the 1480s Lord Howard had a regular arrangement with the landlord William Martin to stable his horses at The Swan.[19]

The Bell's existence is first attested in 1416 when it was described as 'a tenement, shop, tavern, fish stall and grounds called la bell.' It formed part of the estate left by the recently deceased Katherine Cotell, widow of William Cotell. Katherine had also been the owner of The Swan. The Bell stood in Colchester Market[20] in St Nicholas's parish,[21] perhaps near the site of the modern *Café Rouge*.

In 1476/7 John Merell was innkeeper at the Falcon. The names of several other inn and tavern keepers of the second half of the 15th century include Roger Martyn, Felicia Pole, John (or perhaps Thomas) Pelham, John Neulond, John Debon, Henry Thurrok, John Digonson, Thomas Dyster, John Debynham and the wives of Roger Purpyt (Purtepet) and William Blackbourne.[22]

Colchester's School

Throughout the Middle Ages the town had its own school. In 1206 the lord bishop of London granted land and appurtenances in south-west Colchester to one William, son of Benedict. The grant included the advowson of the Church of Our Lady-at-the-

A mediaeval classroom.

Wall, the chapel of St Andrew and the Colchester school. This passing reference proves that at some date prior to 1206 a school had been established in Colchester. The site of this school cannot be precisely located, but it stood somewhere between St Mary's Lane to the north and the lane next to Headgate to the south, and between the town wall (to the west) and Head Street (to the east).[23]

The Colchester school was probably a simple building with a single classroom. The education provided would have been for boys only. There was some debate in mediaeval England concerning the advisability of teaching aristocratic girls to read (this practice was viewed with some favour since it would eventually enable the girls to help their husbands run their family estates). Undoubtedly, however, any teaching of girls would have been confined to the home. Nothing more is heard of the Colchester school in the ensuing centuries, and one might have deduced that it had disappeared were it not for its sudden reappearance in the documentary record in the second half of the 15th century.

This second brief glimpse is fortuitous and is due to the fact that one 15th-century schoolmaster was a man of repulsive habits. The man's name is not preserved, but the Colchester court rolls report that, 'the Master of the schools is in the common habit of casting the dung of his school over and beyond the stone wall of the town at *Le Posterne* and there making a dunghill.' This practice was of course illegal, and in 1463–64 the schoolmaster was fined fourpence for indulging in it (court roll transcripts p.99). Ironically, had this not been the case the continued existence of Colchester's school into the 15th century might have remained unknown. The anonymous schoolmaster's crime confirms the approximate location of the school to just inside the postern gate and to the south of the Church of Our Lady-at-the-Wall. The mediaeval school was thus located not far from Colchester's present sixth-form college.

The Tennis Court

As in the case of the school, the existence of Colchester's mediaeval tennis court is known chiefly as a result of peccadilloes. On 3 September 1463 the household accounts of Sir John Howard record that he reimbursed 4s 1d to Sir William Warner of Ipswich 'for money leyd owht be hym for pleyyng at the tennys'.[24] However, this particular game may have been played not in Colchester but in Ipswich. Nevertheless, there was undoubtedly a tennis court in Colchester in the 14th and 15th centuries,[25] and in 1481 Robert Veer and Richard Knolles were fined 6d. each for playing tennis during divine service.[26] There is no indication as to the location of the tennis court but it may have been in the vicinity of Bere Lane (Vinyard Street) where other recreational facilities such as brothels and bear baiting were provided.

The Colchester tennis court would have been for the playing of 'real tennis', not modern (lawn) tennis. As popularly perceived today, this ancient game comes trailing clouds of courtly and aristocratic glory. The game was played at the Burgundian ducal court and seems to have spread from there to all the courts of Europe. Judging from his surname, one of the men who was fined for playing tennis in Colchester may have been a relative of the earl of Oxford. On the basis of such associations, one might be tempted to envisage the Colchester court as an indoor structure in a well-to-do part of the town catering for an upper-class clientele. Yet the closeness of the relationship (if any) between Richard Veer and the earl of Oxford is unknown and it is certain that his opponent, Knolles, was a working man who was regularly employed by Sir John Howard in the construction of the new chimneys at Howard's Colchester house.[27] Moreover, the fact that in 1425 a Colchester labourer had been prosecuted for being a night vagrant and a tennis player seems to suggest that in 15th-century Colchester this game had a low social profile.[28]

Indeed, although the name 'real tennis' is often said to be an ancient spelling variant for 'royal tennis', it is actually a moot point whether this interpretation is correct. The mediaeval Colchester records simply refer to 'tennis', the name 'real tennis' may be merely a much later invention to distinguish the traditional game from the more recently-evolved 'lawn tennis'. The French name for the old game is perhaps more informative. *Jeu de paume* indicates that this was a game originally played not with a racket but simply with the palm of the hand. This implies that it had very basic origins indeed – more probably in the streets than in royal courts.

Open-air courts for real tennis are known to have existed and so the Colchester tennis court should perhaps be envisaged, therefore, as a simple open-air structure, rather basic in its equipment. We have already seen that its *aficionados* may not have been particularly aristocratic. Thus, the Colchester court may well have been located outside the walls to the south, somewhere near modern Vineyard Street. As we are about to discover, this neighbourhood was a well-known – even notorious – venue for the pursuit of motley pleasures and diversions in Colchester.

Bear Baiting

Mediaeval entertainment included many activities involving animals, which would now be considered brutal and unacceptable by most people. In mediaeval England bulls were baited as an obligatory prelude to their slaughter, since it was thought to make the meat more tender.

More rarely there was also baiting of bears at the bear stake, though by the 15th century bear baiting could only be financed by great and wealthy aristocrats. This was because bears had long been extinct in England, so staging a bear baiting necessitated the importation of a live bear from the European mainland. In modern bear baiting (where this persists) the bear is generally considered too valuable to be killed, so he is only lacerated and scarred by the dogs before being hauled away to fight again another day. It is probable that this was also the case in late mediaeval England, where the fighting bears were a costly imported luxury.

A performing bear.

A simple bear stake could easily be erected on any piece of open ground as no enclosure or building is required. However, in mediaeval England arenas for bear baiting were often created. These were usually known as bear gardens. They consisted of a circular enclosure called the *pit* which was surrounded by high fences, together with raised seats for the spectators. A post was planted in the pit and to this the bear was chained by its leg or neck. This allowed the animal to move with some freedom, but not to escape. Hunting dogs were then incited to attack it. The following 15th-century description of bear baiting with dogs is not an actual report, but describes an imagined event. 'All the yonge folkes of this towne dyde rune yesterday to the castell to se a bere batyde with fers dogges within the wallys. It was greatly to be wondrede, for he dyde defende hymselfe so with hys craftynes and his wyllynes from the cruell doggys methought he sett not a whitt be their woodenes [madness] not by their fersnes.'[29]

At earlier periods the dogs had probably been replaced as they tired or were wounded or killed and the baiting was prolonged. Certainly animals were sometimes baited to death. By the later Middle Ages, however, preserving the life of the valuable bear was probably a prime consideration, which may well have limited the duration of the 'entertainment'. It is known that the bears which figured in such 'entertainment' at Southwark at a slightly later period were well-known to the spectators and had names, so clearly they were not killed, but 'performed' regularly at the bear garden. Moreover, bear baiting did not always involve dogs. One alternative and slightly less appalling form of this 'sport' involved direct human provocation of the bear. In this instance men who kept safely out of reach prodded the tethered animal with sticks while the spectators delighted in its growing frenzy.

Colchester's bear stake was in the mediaeval 'Bere Lane' (or *Berislane*). It seems rather a pity that this ancient street name was supressed in the 19th century in favour of the meaningless 'Vineyard Street' in an attempt to combat immorality,[30] since the continued use of the old name could have served as a kind of memorial to the animals which were once tortured there.

By the 15th century, at least, the bear stake stood in an enclosure of some kind. We know this for certain because in 1473 when John and Margaret Vykery disposed of some property on the west side of St Botolph's Street, the dwelling was described as being adjacent to Lose Brook (see chapter one), while what appears to have been the north-western corner of its enclosed garden backed onto the garden of the Bear Hall (*Berehalle*).[31] Thanks to the Vykery evidence the location of Colchester's Bear Hall garden and bear stake can be fixed with some precision. They must have stood somewhere towards the eastern boundary of the present Osborne Street car park, or perhaps just a little further east, under the buildings which now occupy the area between the car park and St Botolph's Street.

The use of the term bear garden in connection with the Vykery property deal proves for certain that at this period a permanent, fenced area with tiered seating for

Dogs attacking a bear.

spectators existed in Colchester where the baiting of animals could take place. However, the reference to the bear hall is even more intriguing, indicating that the structure was much more than a mere open-air fenced enclosure. It was clearly a building of some kind, perhaps with roofs to protect the spectators from the weather. In late 16th-century Southwark the bear garden and the nearby pit for bull baiting were round or polygonal structures with a central arena for the animals which was open to the elements but which was surrounded by roofed tiers of seating. Maps of the period depict both of the Southwark arenas as substantial three-storey buildings that seem to have been virtually indistinguishable in appearance from contemporary late Elizabethan theatres such as the Globe.[32] These arenas in Southwark certainly existed by about 1560. The date of their construction is unrecorded but they may well have dated from the previous century or even earlier. This raises the intriguing possibility that the 15th-century Colchester Bear Hall may also have been a circular timber-framed building, similar in appearance to the Globe Theatre.

In spite of its name, by the later Middle Ages the Colchester bear stake was actually used mainly for baiting bulls prior to their slaughter. Its last recorded use for baiting a bear had been in 1365,[33] and in 1470/1 there were complaints that *Le*

Berestake was in need of repair.[34] However, it seems possible that it may still have seen occasional use for bear baiting in the 15th century since there were local members of the aristocracy whose household establishments are known to have included the office of bear-ward. The household accounts of Sir John Howard record a few payments in respect of bears. A gold angel was paid to Lord Stanley's bear-ward in November 1463, and a further half angel was paid to a bear-ward in December 1463.[35] The Howard accounts do not make it clear whether the charges of these bear-wards were intended for baiting, or whether they were kept as pets or as dancers. Indeed, given the rather ambivalent mediaeval attitude to animals, it may well be that the bears were pets and dancers and were also baited from time to time.

Brothels

In Southwark the arenas for baiting animals stood in close proximity to the brothels, and this also proves to have been the case in Colchester. In the Middle Ages 'the pleasure of sex was…taken as so self-evident as to require no particular comment. Sexual activity in the form of prostitution was thought to be an evil thing, but at the same time necessary to keep sinful men driven by lust from corrupting respectable women, including their own wives, or from turning to homosexuality'.[36] Attitudes to prostitutes varied over time. It seems that during the 12th and 13th centuries prostitution became accepted, and during the 14th and 15th centuries was institutionalised, becoming subject to regulation. French and Italian towns authorised brothels in defined locations outside the town and then prosecuted illicit prostitution within the town walls or that involving married women. The process began with negative enactments 'defining places where prostitutes should *not* work'. Later 'places of prostitution were reduced to one house,…often the property of the municipality.'[37]

Some English towns and cities followed the continental example in delimiting specific areas within which prostitutes might operate, although in England this seems not to have been a universal practice.[38] In London efforts were made to confine prostitution to defined areas, including Cock Lane and Southwark. 'The city authorities were not so much concerned with personal morality as with keeping the peace.'[39] The Southwark brothels (on land owned by the bishop of Winchester) dated back to at least the 12th century when they were the subject of ordinances laid down by Henry II.[40] Little documentation seems to be available for other English towns and cities, but in Southwark, as we have seen, brothels were sited on property owned by the church;[41] this was also the case elsewhere in Europe. Southwark stewholders had to be male,[42] and were prohibited from beating the women or from lending them money. In some places prostitutes were required to wear specified clothing but this was not the case in Southwark. The Southwark stewholders did not employ the prostitutes, they merely rented them premises from which to work. Rents were high, but this probably made up for the fact that the stewholders got no other cut from the girls' earnings.

There were similar opportunities for recreational sexual activity in Colchester. The town adopted a licensing scheme like those which applied in London and on the Continent. Colchester's licensed brothels were located just outside the town walls on the southern side in 'Bere Lane' (Vineyard Street).[43] Bere Lane was a very deprived area, inhabited by some of the poorest people of Colchester. Some property in Bere Lane was owned in the 15th century by St Botolph's Priory[44] and St John's Abbey,[45] and in the 16th century (and possibly earlier) the borough also owned property there.[46] 'Berislane, was appointed by the by-laws as the proper place for

A mediaeval stews.

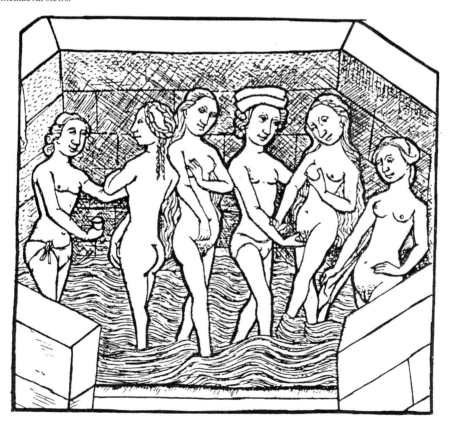

prostitutes,[47] which was why the bailiffs suppressed brothels elsewhere in the town and punished individual prostitutes caught operating outside the permitted zone. The distance between the road and the town wall was narrow here, and houses had little space at the back of them.'[48]

Unsurprisingly, perhaps, the prostitutes did not always confine themselves strictly to their licensed area. There was a crackdown in the 1480s on harlots who were ranging beyond the confines of Bere Lane to operate on nearby St John's Green and loiter around the walls of the abbey.[49] Ample evidence of the prosecution of illicit 15th-century Colchester prostitution survives in the court rolls.[50] In Colchester, as in many other English towns, it seems the women were further controlled and exploited by means of such prosecutions and fines.[51] Evidence of similar prosecutions exist also in nearby Ipswich, suggesting that this kind of exploitation was widespread.[52]

After Bere Lane the poorest part of mediaeval Colchester was probably the area stretching beyond the East Gate, down East Hill and along East Street. It is not surprising to discover therefore that when a purge of illicit brothels was conducted in 1406, two out of the three unlicensed houses were situated there – one managed by a cordwainer, the other by a cordwainer and his partner. The latter, a down-market business, catered for 'wicked and disreputable men and women', whereas the third illicit brothel, which was located in a better quarter of the town, had been visited by priests.[53]

In addition to its authorised and unauthorised brothels, mediaeval Colchester also had a number of freelance prostitutes. This was frowned upon, particularly when it involved married women or the daughters (or the servants) of respectable families. In fact, we know about such women precisely because they were brought before the borough court and fined for their activities. Thus in 1447 we are told 'that the wife of Walter Facoler, and Agnes, wife of John Rodebryght; Margery Sadler; the wife of John Bysshop, butcher; Katherine Straunge; Alice Barbour (*alias* Goldsmyth) and her mother, Margaret; and the wife of William Talworth are common pimps and prostitutes, practising prostitution.'[54]

In spite of fines and adverse publicity the problem continued. Twenty years later it was reported that 'Katherine, wife of Henry Mildwell, is in the common habit of receiving into her house by night a certain John Byrde, tailor, in a suspicious manner'.[55] In the same year 'Richard Coker is in the common habit of practising harlotry with John Knok's wife, whereby strifes and quarrels are nightly made', while Thomas Kechyn junior was practising harlotry with William Sayer's wife. Richard

Tynker supported common harlots in his house (thereby turning it into an unlicensed brothel) and William Hauteyn junior was committing harlotry with a common prostitute called Alice whose surname is not recorded,[56] though she may perhaps have been Alice Waterfalle who would later be cited for her habitual adultery with the rector of St Nicholas's Church.[57] Ten years on we find Joan, wife of Geoffrey Picard, denounced as a common strumpet and procuress (she was fined half a gold angel),[58] while in 1481 Thomas Davy fell foul of the law for committing adultery with John Perkyn's wife, as well as debauching various other men's maidservants.[59] These records of such prosecutions bring us into very intimate contact with some of the individuals who made up the mediaeval population of Colchester.

Notes

1. BL, Add. MS 46349, f. 138r; *HHB*, part 1, p. 400.

2. Soc. Ant., MS 77, f. 12r; *HHB*, part 2, p. 300.

3. Britnell, *Colchester in the Fifteenth Century – a Portrait*. Britnell cites the largest number of innkeepers fined at once for baking bread (at Hocktide in 1400): ERO D/B5 Cr31, m. 18r, and also the number of vintners fined for breaking the law on several occasions in the early 15th century: ERO D/B5 Cr32, mm. 2r, 9r, 15d; Cr34, m. 2r; Cr43, m. 20r.

4. Soc. Ant., MS 77, f. 26r; *HHB*, part 2, p. 327.

5. ERO D/B5 Cr61, m. 8v.

6. It might be supposed that some tavern keepers maintained more than one tavern (so that the total number of taverns could have been higher). However, the fact that John Fleccher was merely a tenant of John Rouge, but was still listed as a tavern keeper in his own right, seems to rule out this possibility.

7. J.A. Jephcott, *The Inns, Taverns and Pubs of Colchester* (Colchester: Bowcott 1995) p. 254.

8. Jephcott notes one other extant pub (The Stockwell Arms) whose *building* dates, in part, from the 15th century, but it is not known to have been in use as a pub earlier than the 19th century: Jephcott, *Inns*, p. 250.

9. North side of High Street. Site now occupied by Angel Court.

10. Extant in Crouch Street.

11. Later 'Queen Elizabeth's Head' and then 'The Cups'. North side of High Street, between the Town Hall and St Peter's churchyard.

12. Extant.

13. Near (behind?) The White Hert (*qv.*) in Helle Lane. Possibly identical with the later 'Swan with two necks' which fronted onto Headgate Street.

14. South side of High Street, near the present Bank Passage.

15. Jephcott, *Inns*, p. 254.

16. ERO, D/B5 Cr72, m. 23v (transcript, p. 120).

17. ERO, D/B5 Cr79, m. 1v (transcript, p. 6).

18. Jephcott, *Inns*, p. 94. The Bull continued to offer stabling facilities until at least the 1920s. P. Denney, *The Changing Face of Colchester* (Derby: Breedon, 2002), p. 43. For *groats* see below, appendix 1.

19. Soc. Ant., MS 76, f. 108v; *HHB*, part 2, p. 150.

20. 'From an ancient order of the city [*sic*] fathers we learn that "the pease and roote market with the onions, garlick and cucumbers shall be holden and kept from the Lyon downwards towards St Nicholas Church and in no other place."'G. Morgan, *The Romance of Essex Inns* (Letchworth: Letchworth Printers, 1963), p. 38.

21. Jephcott, *Inns*, pp. 75, 254, 290 & *passim*.

22. ERO, D/B5 Cr73, m. 27v (transcript, p. 133); Cr76, m. 11v (transcript, p. 66/7); Cr77, m. 2r (transcript, p. 7); Cr79, m. 1v (transcript, p. 6).

23. J.H. Round, *Register of the Scholars admitted to the Colchester School 1637–1740*, Colchester 1897, p. i; R.E.G. Kirk, ed., *Feet of Fines for Essex, 1182-1272*, Essex Archaeological Society 1899–1910, vol. 1, p. 39.

24. BL, Add. MS 46349, f. 48r; *HHB*, part 1, p. 221.

25. Tennis in Colchester is first mentioned in 1382. VCH, *Essex*, vol. 9, p. 63, citing ERO, D/B5 Cr21, m. 30.

26. ERO, D/B5 Cr79, m. 1v (transcript, p. 6). Records of the Colchester tennis court date back to at least 1425, see VCH, *Essex*, vol. 9, p. 63.

27. See for example, Soc. Ant., MS 76, f. 95r; MS 77, f. 51r; *HHB*, part 2, pp. 122, 378. The house in question is now the Red Lion Hotel.

28. VCH, *Essex*, vol. 9, p. 63, citing the Colchester court rolls.

29. Text prepared for Latin translation by a 15th-century schoolmaster at Magdalen School, Oxford, quoted in C. Reeves, *Pleasures and Pastimes in Mediaeval England*, Stroud 1997, p. 101.

30. The 19th-century renaming was an attempt to rid the road of its unsavoury reputation which stemmed from its longstanding link with prostitution (see below: 'Brothels').

31. ERO, D/B5 Cr75, m. 7v (transcript, p. 43).

32. A. Prockter and R. Taylor, *The A to Z of Elizabethan London*, London 1979, pp. 22, 24, 32.

33. VCH, *Essex*, vol. 9, p. 63, citing the Colchester court rolls.

34. ERO, D/B5 Cr74, m. 23r (transcript, p. 87).

35. BL, Add. MS 46349, f. 5r & v; *HHB*, part 1, pp. 156, 157.

36. Reeves, *Pleasures and Pastimes*, p. 204.

37. L.L. Otis, *Prostitution in Mediaeval Society* (Chicago and London: University of Chicago Press, 1985), pp. 15–39, 111–113.

38. R.M. Karras, *Common Women* (Oxford: OUP 1996), pp. 35–43.

39. D.W. Robertson, *Chaucer's London* (New York: John Wiley & Sons, 1968), pp. 101–04.

40. A. McCall, *The Mediaeval Underworld* (London: H. Hamilton, 1979), pp. 182–85.

41. McCall, *The Mediaeval Underworld*, pp. 182–83.

42. 'Stews' were originally bath-houses, but in 15th-century England the word always means 'brothels'.

43. VCH, *Essex*, vol. 9, p. 228, notes that this area was popularly known as 'Harlots' Row' in the 19th and early 20th centuries. J.B. Harvey, *Colchester Street Names*, [no place of publication] 1889, explains that the new name of 'Vineyard Street' was invented about the middle of the 19th century because the area still had a 'notoriously bad character' at that period.

44. B.*OB*, pp. 88, 208.

45. In 1476 Robert Cosyn and his wife Joan (*née* Fuller) owned a house on the south side of *Bereslane* (Vineyard Street) which adjoined a garden belonging to St John's Abbey: ERO, D/B5 Cr76, transcript p. 175.

46. VCH, *Essex*, vol. 9, p. 103: 'in 1458-9 the borough chamberlain was unable to collect rents from unoccupied houses…in Bere Lane' (Vineyard Street).

47. Britnell, citing CR 19/10r; CR 20/11r.

48. Britnell.

49. ERO, D/B5 Cr79, m. 1v (transcript, p. 6), refers to the fining of a group of *comunes pimbiis…manens apud murum Sancti Iohannis*.

50. See, for example, ERO, D/B5 Cr61, m. 15r, and Cr72, m. 11v (transcript, p. 56).

51. Compare the evidence of the careers of mediaeval English prostitutes in Karras, *Common Women*, p. 66 and *passim*.

52. IRO, C/2/8/3/1, Frankpledge Roll, 13 June 1508. This lists a number of *meretrices* and their male associates (brothel keepers and those who act as pimps). The roll insists on the fact that the women were married (possibly implying that they should be respectable) and that their offences were committed *infra libertatem ville*.

53. Britnell, citing CR 36/2r,d. Britnell believes that the John Bysshop who had a share in the second of these brothels was the John Bysshop, junior, cordwainer, who occurs in 1405: CR 34/15r.

54. ERO, D/B5 Cr61, m. 15r. The original text is in Latin.

55. ERO, D/B5 Cr73, m. 18v (transcript, p. 89).

56. ERO, D/B5 Cr73, mm. 18v, 27r (transcript, pp. 91, 129, 132, 133).

57. ERO, D/B5 Cr79, m. 1v (transcript, p. 6).

58. ERO, D/B5 Cr76, m. 2v (transcript, p. 9).

59. ERO, D/B5 Cr78, m. 10r (transcript, p. 46).

MEDIAEVAL COLCESTRIANS

One of the key lost features of mediaeval Colchester is, in fact, its colourful human population. A list of names of all the men living in Colchester in 1471–72 is reproduced in appendix 2, and this is almost as good as a census of the town's late mediaeval male population. By itself, such a list supplies little more than names, but in many cases, as we have already seen, it is possible to add further details to flesh out the bones of those long-dead. However, since many of these details are derived from Colchester's mediaeval court rolls they do not always show the inhabitants at their best!

Some mediaeval Colcestrians bore well-known modern surnames like, for example, Dover or Plummer (though, of course, mediaeval spelling was often variable). Surnames such as Boleyn and Wolsey, which were to become well-known in the Tudor period, also appear in mediaeval Colchester records. However, there are also surnames such as Flyngaunt and Raumdewe which have subsequently disappeared entirely. Whatever became of mediaeval Colchester's once numerous

Raumdewes? Presumably they just died out, or, at least, produced only daughters and no sons so that their surname disappeared. The origin of some surnames, like Dover and Shipman, is obvious, but names like Flyngaunt are not so apparent. And what should we make of Drinkmelk? Was this originally intended as an insult – somewhat akin to describing someone as a milksop?

Women are named in the mediaeval records less frequently than men. Colchester had large numbers of female brewers who were listed annually. However, they figure

Male head from the south side of the Abbey Gatehouse.

not under their own names but simply as 'the wife of...' or 'the widow of...'. Named women do sometimes figure in property deals and bequests, but otherwise they tend to be identified only when they were in trouble. This most frequently occurred when they were accused of sexual misconduct. The names of many mediaeval Colchester women are preserved only because they were said to be harlots.

However, in 1466–67 we encounter the mysterious Jeweyn Blakecote of St Martin's parish who was a fortune-teller (*sortilega*).[1] Clearly she was not a very good one as she apparently failed to foresee her own forthcoming prosecution and fine for activities which, to the mediaeval mind, probably seemed dangerously close to the black arts. We also find women who were fined for tittle-tattle and gossip. Jeweyn Blakecote was a scandal-monger as well as a fortune-teller, but her hefty fine of half a gold angel must have been due mainly to her fortune-telling activities because at the same court Benedicta Hill, who was another 'scold and gossip' (but evidently not a fortune-teller), got off with the much lighter fine of 3d. Even being a tittle-tattler did not always guarantee that a woman would be recorded under her own name. We never discover the real names of the wives of Thomas Benale and Roger Tyler, who were accused of spying on their neighbours and eavesdropping.[2]

Some local dynasties, such as the Flyngaunts, were well-established in Colchester by the 15th century. The Flyngaunts worked in the cloth trade and their extended family remained close-knit as we find Flyngaunt cousins helping one another out on various occasions. Richard and Alice Flyngaunt were the executors of John Flyngaunt junior's will, while Thomas Flyngaunt acted as their pledge when they brought a court case relating to this will.[3] Later, Thomas and John Flyngaunt stood pledge for Prior John Flyngaunt of St Botolph's Priory.[4] There are many similar instances of mutual support within this family.[5] The Flyngaunts owned property just outside the town walls, on East Street (modern East Hill) and possibly also within the walls near the castle in Frere Street.

The Lalleford family was much less numerous than the Flyngaunts, and appears not to have originated in Colchester. Thomas Lalleford had been born in Sudbury,[6] and it seems probable that a family of this surname moved from Suffolk to Colchester around the middle of the 15th century. Three male Lallefords are mentioned in the Colchester court rolls: Thomas, Richard and John. The family served Sir John (later Lord) Howard who had a house in Colchester (now the Red Lion Inn) and who was constable of Colchester Castle. The Lallefords are regularly mentioned in his household accounts.

Female head from the south side of All Saints' Church.

Like the Flyngaunts, the Lallefords also supported one another. In 1473–74 Richard and John Lalleford acted as guarantors for Thomas Lalleford in a court case.[7] Later, in 1476–77 Thomas stood guarantee for Richard Lalleford,[8] and in another case Richard stood pledge for Thomas.[9] Richard was probably Thomas's brother, and John, their father. Certainly John belonged to an older generation than Thomas and Richard. His name occurs in the court rolls from the mid-1440s.[10] At that period he is described as a smith.[11] By the 1460s he is called a brasier.[12] John's wife was called Agnes, and she brewed and sold beer.[13] They lived in Head Ward[14] and in addition to two sons they also had at least one daughter whose name, however, is unknown.[15]

Sir John Howard was a significant figure in Colchester society in the second half of the 15th century, patronising various Colchester suppliers. Among these were members of the Beche family. On 28 November 1465 Howard acquired 'a garnish of counterfeit vessels' from Beche of Colchester.[16] A 'garnish' comprised a dozen platters, a dozen dishes and a dozen saucers, all made of pewter. John Beche was a member of an established Colchester family who probably shared Howard's Yorkist sympathies, for John Beche's forebears had been loyal to Richard II and had been involved in an early plot to dethrone the Lancastrian usurper Henry IV.[17] Unfortunately the Beche family's predilection for the first name 'John' makes it rather difficult to distinguish one family member from another, but the John Beche who figures in the Colchester court roll in 1466–67 is probably identical with Howard's supplier, though he is described there not as a pewterer but as a cardmaker.[18] Earlier in the 15th century the name John Beche had figured in the list of Colchester bailiffs in 10 years spanning from 1428 to 1456. In 1456 John Beche died during his period of office as bailiff. It is possible that these entries, covering a total span of 28 years, all refer to a single individual who might have been the father or the grandfather of John Howard's pewterer.

Further evidence of Beche family involvement in the manufacture of pewter in Colchester emerges from records of the Lawhundred held in the town

Pectoral Cross of Abbot Beche, last abbot of Colchester.

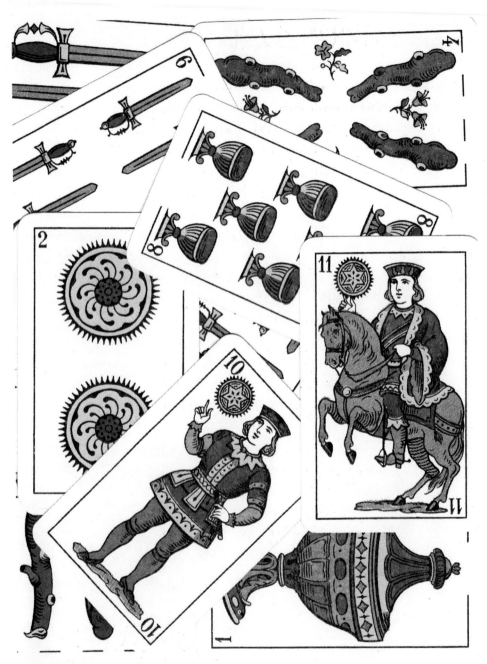

Mediaeval-style playing cards.

on the Monday after the Feast of St Michael the Archangel, 6 Edward IV [6 October 1466]. On this occasion William Beche was fined for selling substandard pewterware. While the court roll does not explicitly state that William Beche had himself made the illicit artefacts, the presumption seems strongly in favour of his having done so. This evidence that the Beche family was probably manufacturing pewterware in Colchester as early as 1465–66 is significant since it antedates by nine years the earliest previously published evidence of pewter manufacture in the town.

The last abbot of Colchester, Abbot Thomas Beche (*alias* Marshall), was probably a descendant of Lord Howard's Beches. Indeed, the abbot may well have known Lord Howard as a boy. Later, like Howard's own descendants, Abbot Beche opposed the religious policy of Henry VIII and was put to death for the stand he took. Abbot Beche's gold pectoral cross, which he was wearing at the time of his execution (probably at the abbey gallows in Greenstead) is now considered a martyr's relic. It is currently in the keeping of the Benedictine Abbey of Buckfast, Devon, 'until St John's Abbey in Colchester is restored'.

During the 1460s Sir John Howard patronised exclusively a single Colchester shoemaker: James the Cordwainer of Colchester.[19] 'James' was probably this man's first name and his surname is unfortunately not recorded. While James was clearly not the only shoemaker in Colchester, he apparently enjoyed the exclusive patronage

After vespers: a modern congregation in St John's Abbey Gatehouse.

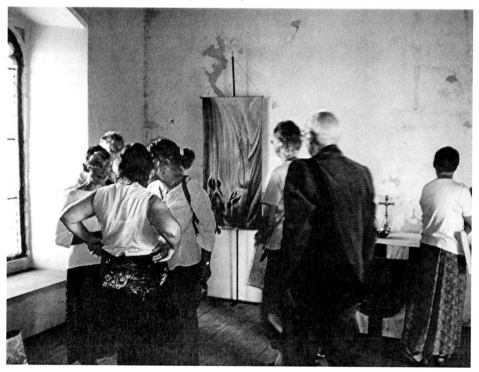

of the Howard family. On several occasions Howard must have been particularly pleased with James's work, for not only did the family continue to employ him but he also received small tips from them in addition to his payments.[20] His footwear ranged in price from 4d for a pair of shoes for Howard's eldest daughter, Isabelle, to 2s 4d paid by Sir John for what was obviously a rather special pair of boots for himself.[21]

The Howard household also bought clothes and armour in Colchester. Clothing was purchased from (among others) Oliver van Cache, who was probably Flemish (or of Flemish descent) and whose wife's name was Isabel.[22] A number of people of Dutch or Flemish origin lived in Colchester in the later Middle Ages, and were admitted to the freedom of the town.[23] Oliver van Cache supplied hosiery, made gowns and repaired garments for the Howard household over a period of some 20 years.[24] John Howard's own costly armour was made in London or in the Low Countries, but cheaper defensive clothing, called 'brigandines' or 'breganders' made of leather and reinforced with metal plates, was certainly made in Colchester for Howard's men-at-arms. For example, on 7 October 1463 a payment of 4d to John Brown, 'armerer' or 'bregander makere', was recorded.[25] The substitution of 'bregander makere' for the more prestigious-sounding 'armerer' in the duplicate copy of this entry implies, perhaps, that Brown's skills were somewhat basic, but elsewhere he is certainly described as an armourer.[26]

Notes

1. ERO, D/B5 Cr73, m. 1v (transcript, p. 7).

2. ERO, D/B5 Cr73, m. 2r (transcript, p. 10).

3. ERO, D/B5 Cr75, m. 22v (transcript, p. 127).

4. ERO, D/B5 Cr80, m. 27v (transcript, p. 96).

5. Thomas and John Flyngaunt stood pledge for Prior John again in 1484/5: ERO, D/B5 Cr81, m. 29r (transcript, p. 99). Thomas Flyngaunt stood pledge for William Flyngaunt on more that one occasion: ERO, D/B5 Cr76, mm. 15v, 16r (transcript, p. 88).

6. His place of birth is noted in connection with his admission as a Colchester burgess in 1471–72: B.OB, p. 125; OB, f. 98r.

7. ERO, D/B5 Cr75, m. 22v (transcript, p. 126).

8. ERO, D/B5 Cr76, m. 3v (transcript, p. 19).

9. ERO, D/B5 Cr76, m. 10v (transcript, p. 61).

10. ERO, D/B5 Cr61, mm. 8v, 9v, 10r, 10v, 11r.

11. ERO, D/B5 Cr61, m. 10r.

12. B.*OB*, p. 125; *OB*, f. 98r.

13. B.*OB*, p. 125; *OB*, f. 98r; ERO, D/B5 Cr61, m. 8v.

14. ERO, D/B5 Cr61, m. 8v.

15. In 1463 an unnamed daughter of John Lalleford was fined 12d. for being a common harlot: ERO, D/B5 Cr72, m 1v (transcript, p. 8).

16. BL, Add. MS 46349, f. 91v; *HHB*, part 1, p. 317.

17. VCH, *Essex*, vol. 9, p. 25.

18. ERO, D/B5 CR 73, m. 1v (transcript, p. 3), where he figures as a juryman.

19. For a detailed analysis of Howard's purchase of footwear, see J. Ashdown-Hill, 'The client network, connections and patronage of Sir John, Lord Howard, first Duke of Norfolk, in north east Essex and south Suffolk', unpublished PhD thesis, University of Essex 2008, appendix 14.

20. BL, Add. MS 46349, ff. 67r, 90v; *HHB*, part 1, pp. 262, 314.

21. 14 July 1464: BL, Add. MS 46349, ff. 66v, 72v; *HHB*, part 1, pp. 261, 274. A pair of boots for Howard usually cost about a shilling.

22. Isabel van Cache issued a deed in favour of William Clopton and others in 1488–89 (B.*OB*, p. 137).

23. See Ashdown-Hill, thesis, section 4.

24. BL, Add. MS 46349, ff. 67r, 72r, 92v, Soc. Ant. MS 76, ff. 118v, 141r, Soc. Ant. MS 77, f. 43r; *HHB*, part 1, pp. 263, 274, 319; part 2, pp. 165, 199, 359.

25. BL, Add. MS 46349, ff. 50r, 53r; *HHB*, part 1, pp. 226, 231.

26. ERO, D/B5 Cr81, mm. 4v, 5v (transcript, pp. 13, 19): case of Sir Laurence Reynsforth *versus* John Brown, armourer. John Brown is probably the John Bron named in both the 1472 Colchester Fealty list (appendix 2), and in an Oath Book entry for 1475, where his wife's name is given as Mathilda (B.*OB*, p. 130).

MEDIAEVAL MYSTERIES

Our exploration of the lost landmarks of mediaeval Colchester is now almost at an end. Hopefully many hitherto unknown facets of the town and its inhabitants have emerged, and some notions of the town's late mediaeval appearance and lifestyle have been revealed. However, mediaeval Colchester still retains some mysteries. The court rolls contain references to mysterious items called *whirlegigges*. What these were is unknown. The University of Michegan's online mediaeval English dictionary can only hazard a guess that a *whirlegigge* was probably 'a rotating device, perhaps a treading wheel used to wind things up into a tower'.[1] As guesses go this seems a reasonable suggestion, but the Colchester *whirlegigges* were to be found in the streets of the town, so they seem unlikely to have been treadmills.

Clearly *whirlegigges* were regarded as intrusive as they became the subjects of prosecutions and this is why we know about them. Thus the Colchester court roll for 1470/1 accuses in forthright (if polyglot) tones *quod iohanes janyn situavit in regia via unam stipidem unius whirlegigge, altitudinus unius manipuli*.[2] Despite the fact that the clerk who wrote this record knew no Latin term for *whirlegigge*, his Latin is in other respects clear and correct. It translates 'that John Janyn placed in the king's street a post of a whirlegigge the height of a maniple'.

No doubt the clerk knew exactly what he was talking about. Sadly, we now have not the faintest idea. Nevertheless, John Janyn's was not an isolated offence. Thirteen years later the rector of All Saints was also in trouble for having a *whirlegigge* on the king's highway.[3] Clearly the occasional *whirlegigge* (whatever that may have been) was a recognised feature of the mediaeval Colchester townscape!

Notes

1.   http://quod.lib.umich.edu/m/med/

2.   ERO, D/B5 Cr74, m. 14v (transcript, p. 58).

3.   ERO, D/B5 Cr80, m. 20r (transcript, pp. 66–67).

APPENDICES

Appendix 1
English mediaeval coinage

Mediaeval England had no bronze or copper coins. The main coin in circulation was the silver penny, abbreviated to 'd' - standing for the Latin *denarius*. This was a thin silver coin roughly 1cm in diameter, which bore a crowned bust facing forward, and supposedly represented the reigning monarch (though all the kings from Edward I to Henry VII actually look identical on their coins). The reverse (tail side) of the silver penny bore a cross. There were similar (but smaller) ½d and ¼d coins (the ¼ pennies were called 'farthings'). The next coins up from the silver penny were the silver 2d, or half-groat, and the silver 4d, or groat. The groat was first introduced by Edward I and became a regular part of the coinage in the reign of Edward III. Its name derived from the French word *gros*, and roughly meant 'a big one'.

In the early Middle Ages only silver coins existed, but Edward I tentatively experimented with the introduction of a gold coin and Edward III made gold coins a fixed part of the English system. For most of the 15th century the main gold coin was the *noble*, worth 80 silver pennies (with half-nobles at 40d and quarter-nobles at 20d). There is some evidence from the household accounts of John Howard (later first Duke of Norfolk) that the gold quarter-noble was known as a *crown*.[1]

Mediaeval money (pennies, half-groat, groat and angel).

However, the coinage of the Yorkist period was different. Edward IV reformed the coinage, abolishing the gold noble and its divisions and introducing a new coin of the same size and weight called the *ryal* (royal), or the *rose noble*, valued at 120d, together with its half and quarter (though no *ryals* were issued during the reigns of Edward V or Richard III). Later Edward IV introduced a new gold coin called the *angel* because it bore a design of the Archangel Michael killing the dragon. This had the same value as the old noble (80d), but it was a coin of much lighter weight containing less gold. There were also half-angels called *angelets* (40d). No other coins existed in the English system until Henry VII introduced further changes at the end of the 15th century. It is important to realise this, because although 15th-century accounts often refer to *shillings* (12d), *marks* (160d or 2 angels) and *pounds* (240d) no coins of these denominations existed, and shillings, marks and pounds were merely 'money of account'.

Summary of the English coinage from Edward III to Henry VI

4d = 1 groat	80d (or 20 groats) = 1 noble
Silver coins:	¼d; ½d; 1d; 2d (half-groat); 4d (groat)
Gold coins:	20d (¼ noble); 40d (½ noble); 80d (noble)

Summary of the English coinage under the Yorkist kings

4d = 1 groat	80d (or 20 groats) = 1 angel; 120d (or 30 groats) = 1 ryal
Silver coins:	¼d; ½d; 1d; 2d (half-groat); 4d (groat)
Gold coins:	30d (¼ ryal); 40d (angelet); 60d (½ ryal); 80d (angel); 120d (ryal)

Appendix 2
List of Mediaeval Colchester Inhabitants

There were no regular census records of the population taken in England in the Middle Ages. However, the mediaeval *Red Paper Book of Colchester* contains a list of men dwelling in the town who swore fealty to the restored Edward IV in 1472. This is presumably a fairly complete list of Colchester's adult male inhabitants at that time[2] and so is therefore a good place to start looking if you want to know who lived in 15th-century Colchester, or if you have mediaeval Colchester ancestors. No women are listed. The original list is divided into 'inhabitants' (i.e. Colcestrians) and 'foreigners' (those who came originally from outside Colchester). Here the list is reproduced in alphabetical order of surnames.[3] The list contains 574 names. The page numbers in the last column refer to W. Gurney Benham's published transcript of the *Red Paper Book*, while the folio numbers refer to the original manuscript.

...	John		Colcestrian	p. 82 / f. 246v
...	Henry		foreigner	p. 83 / f. 249v
...hanteyn	...	(senior)	Colcestrian	p. 82 / f. 247r
Abbott	John		foreigner	p. 83 / f. 249v
Ailemere	Henry		foreigner	p. 83 / f. 248v
Akent	John		foreigner	p. 83 / f. 248v
Aldeham	John		foreigner	p. 83 / f. 248v
Algood	Ralph		Colcestrian	p. 82 / f. 246v
Algood	John		foreigner	p. 83 / f. 248r
Algood	John		foreigner	p. 83 / f. 249r
Alstyn	John		foreigner	p. 83 / f. 249r
Alye	William		Colcestrian	p. 82 / f. 246v
Andrew	John	plumber	Colcestrian	p. 82 / f. 247r
Ansell	Rihes.		foreigner	p. 83 / f. 249r
Arketill	Henry		foreigner	p. 83 / f. 249r
Armerer	John		foreigner	p. 83 / f. 248v
Arnold	John		foreigner	p. 83 / f. 248r
Artour	Stephen		foreigner	p. 83 / f. 248r
Assheman	John		Colcestrian	p. 82 / f. 246v
Asshman	Richard		foreigner	p. 82 / f. 247v
Austyn	John	(senior)	foreigner	p. 83 / f. 248r
Austyn	Henry		foreigner	p. 83 / f. 249r
Awbre	William		foreigner	p. 82 / f. 247v
Ayston	Richard		Colcestrian	p. 81 / f. 246r
Bacon	Thomas		Colcestrian	p. 82 / f. 246v
Baker	Walter		Colcestrian	p. 82 / f. 247r
Baker	Walter		foreigner	p. 83 / f. 248v
Baldewyn	Robert	(junior)	foreigner	p. 82 / f. 247v
Baldewyn	John		foreigner	p. 84 / f. 249v
Baldry	John		foreigner	p. 82 / f. 247v
Baley	John	butcher	foreigner	p. 83 / f. 249v
Ball	John		foreigner	p. 83 / f. 248r
Ball	Richard		foreigner	p. 83 / f. 249r
Balsham	John		foreigner	p. 83 / f. 248r
Bantone	Robert		foreigner	p. 83 / f. 248v
Banyng	William		foreigner	p. 83 / f. 248r
Barbour	William		foreigner	p. 82 / f. 247v
Barbour	John		foreigner	p. 82 / f. 247v
Barbour	Richard		foreigner	p. 83 / f. 248v
Bardolf	John		Colcestrian	p. 81 / f. 246r
Barford	Robert		Colcestrian	p. 82 / f. 247r
Barker	Robert		Colcestrian	p. 81 / f. 246r
Barker	Thomas		Colcestrian	p. 82 / f. 247r
Barker	Robert	(junior)	foreigner	p. 83 / f. 248v
Barker	John		foreigner	p. 83 / f. 248v
Barker	Thomas		foreigner	p. 83 / f. 248v
Barker	John		foreigner	p. 83 / f. 249r
Barker	Peter		foreigner	p. 83 / f. 249v
Barly	William		Colcestrian	p. 81 / f. 246v
Baron	John	carpenter	Colcestrian	p. 82 / f. 246v
Baron	John		Colcestrian	p. 82 / f. 247r

Bassam	Richard		Colcestrian	p. 82 / f. 246v
Bawde	William		Colcestrian	p. 81 / f. 246v
Bawdewyn	Robert		foreigner	p. 83 / f. 248v
Beche	John	cardmaker	Colcestrian	p. 82 / f. 246v
Beche	William		foreigner	p. 83 / f. 249r
Bedford	John		foreigner	p. 82 / f. 247v
Belle	John		foreigner	p. 82 / f. 247v
Bernard	Robert		foreigner	p. 84 / f. 249v
Bernard	William		Colcestrian	p. 82 / f. 247r
Berte	John		foreigner	p. 82 / f. 248r
Bertelet	John		foreigner	p. 83 / f. 249r
Berwik	Thomas		foreigner	p. 83 / f. 249r
Berwyk	Richard		Colcestrian	p. 82 / f. 246v
Besewik	Thomas		foreigner	p. 83 / f. 249r
Bette	Roger		foreigner	p. 83 / f. 248v
Bette	John		foreigner	p. 83 / f. 249r
Bierbrewer	Henry		foreigner	p. 83 / f. 248v
Bieste	John		foreigner	p. 83 / f. 249r
Blackbourne	William		Colcestrian	p. 81 / f. 246r
Blak	Simon		Colcestrian	p. 82 / f. 246v
Blaxton	William		Colcestrian	p. 82 / f. 246v
Blomvelde	John		Colcestrian	p. 82 / f. 246v
Blower	John		foreigner	p. 83 / f. 248r
Bloy	Nicholas		foreigner	p. 82 / f. 247v
Bloye	William		Colcestrian	p. 82 / f. 247r
Bolt	William		foreigner	p. 82 / f. 247v
Bone	Richard		foreigner	p. 82 / f. 248r
Bonefant	William		foreigner	p. 83 / f. 249v
Bonere[4]	Laurence		foreigner	p. 82 / f. 247v
Boteler	William		foreigner	p. 82 / f. 247v
Bradford	John		foreigner	p. 82 / f. 247v
Bradlee	Henry		Colcestrian	p. 82 / f. 247r
Brady	Robert		foreigner	p. 83 / f. 248r
Brandmere	Thomas		foreigner	p. 82 / f. 247v
Bregge	Henry		foreigner	p. 83 / f. 248v
Breton	Peter		Colcestrian	p. 82 / f. 246v
Bright	William		foreigner	p. 83 / f. 248r
Brome	Thomas		Colcestrian	p. 81 / f. 246r
Bron	John		foreigner	p. 82 / f. 247v
Bron	William		foreigner	p. 83 / f. 248r
Bron	Peter		foreigner	p. 83 / f. 248v
Bron	Thomas		foreigner	p. 83 / f. 248v
Brondale	Richard		foreigner	p. 83 / f. 248r
Brook	Thomas		Colcestrian	p. 81 / f. 246v
Brook	Thomas		foreigner	p. 83 / f. 249r
Brown	William		foreigner	p. 83 / f. 249v
Brownyng	Richard		foreigner	p. 83 / f. 249r
Brunde[l]	Peter		Colcestrian	p. 82 / f. 246v
Bryan	John		Colcestrian	p. 82 / f. 246v
Bryon	William		foreigner	p. 83 / f. 249v
Buk	William		foreigner	p. 82 / f. 247v

Bukkenham	Robert		foreigner	p. 83 / f. 248r
Bukworth	John		foreigner	p. 83 / f. 249r
Bullok	Thomas		foreigner	p. 83 / f. 249r
Burton	John		Colcestrian	p. 82 / f. 246v
Burton	Nicholas		Colcestrian	p. 82 / f. 247r
Burton	William		foreigner	p. 83 / f. 249r
Bussh	John		foreigner	p. 83 / f. 249r
Cach, van	Oliver		foreigner	p. 82 / f. 248r
Caley	William		foreigner	p. 83 / f. 248r
Calgh	Robert		Colcestrian	p. 82 / f. 247r
Cambyle	John		Colcestrian	p. 82 / f. 246v
Capelyn	John	tiler	foreigner	p. 83 / f. 249r
Carre	Roger		foreigner	p. 82 / f. 247v
Carter	John	pedlar	Colcestrian	p. 82 / f. 247r
Cely	James		Colcestrian	p. 82 / f. 246v
Chanseys	Harry		foreigner	p. 83 / f. 249v
Chapman	John		Colcestrian	p. 81 / f. 246v
Chapman	Richard		Colcestrian	p. 82 / f. 247r
Chatele	Robert		Colcestrian	p. 82 / f. 246v
Chirchman	… [John?]		Colcestrian	p. 82 / f. 247r
Clayson	Thomas		Colcestrian	p. 82 / f. 247r
Clere	Nicholas		Colcestrian	p. 81 / f. 246r
Clerk	John	carter	Colcestrian	p. 82 / f. 246v
Clerk	John	chandeler	foreigner	p. 83 / f. 248v
Cleveland	Robert		foreigner	p. 83 / f. 248r
Clovier	John		foreigner	p. 82 / f. 247v
Cobbe	John		foreigner	p. 83 / f. 248r
Cok	Robert		foreigner	p. 83 / f. 249r
Cole	John		foreigner	p. 83 / f. 248v
Cole	John	(senior)	foreigner	p. 83 / f. 249v
Cole	John	(junior)	foreigner	p. 84 / f. 249v
Colvelle	John		foreigner	p. 83 / f. 249v
Colyn	John		Colcestrian	p. 81 / f. 246r
Cook	John	plumber	Colcestrian	p. 81 / f. 246v
Cook	Richard		Colcestrian	p. 82 / f. 246v
Cook	John		foreigner	p. 82 / f. 247v
Coubregge	Walter		foreigner	p. 83 / f. 249r
Coubregge	Robert		foreigner	p. 83 / f. 249r
Cowper	Richard		Colcestrian	p. 81 / f. 246v
Crake	John		foreigner	p. 83 / f. 249r
Crakebone	Thomas		Colcestrian	p. 82 / f. 247r
Crane	William		foreigner	p. 83 / f. 248v
Cranemere	Richard		foreigner	p. 82 / f. 248r
Cremere	John		Colcestrian	p. 82 / f. 247r
Cristofre	John		Colcestrian	p. 81 / f. 246v
Cristofre	Robert		foreigner	p. 82 / f. 248r
Crosse	John		foreigner	p. 83 / f. 248v
Crowe	John		Colcestrian	p. 82 / f. 247r
Crowe	John		foreigner	p. 83 / f. 248v
Culpak	William		Colcestrian	p. 82 / f. 247r
Curde	Roger		foreigner	p. 83 / f. 248v

Curteys	...		Colcestrian	p. 82 / f. 247r
Curteys	Robert		foreigner	p. 83 / f. 248r
Curteys	Richard		foreigner	p. 83 / f. 249v
Da...	Thomas		foreigner	p. 83 / f. 248v
Dale	William		Colcestrian	p. 81 / f. 246r
Damet	John		Colcestrian	p. 82 / f. 247r
Dashom	William		Colcestrian	p. 81 / f. 246v
Davy	William		Colcestrian	p. 81 / f. 246r
Dean	William		Colcestrian	p. 82 / f. 246v
Dear	William		foreigner	p. 82 / f. 247v
Debon	John		Colcestrian	p. 82 / f. 246v
Debynham	[John?]		foreigner	p. 82 / f. 248r
Derwynde	John		foreigner	p. 83 / f. 248v
Deth	Robert		Colcestrian	p. 82 / f. 246v
Deth	John		foreigner	p. 84 / f. 249v
Diker	William		Colcestrian	p. 82 / f. 247r
Dowale	William		Colcestrian	p. 82 / f. 247r
Dowale	Leman(?)		foreigner	p. 82 / f. 247v
Dowe	William		Colcestrian	p. 82 / f. 247r
Downyng	Robert		Colcestrian	p. 82 / f. 247r
Drynkmelk	John		Colcestrian	p. 82 / f. 247r
Duches	John		foreigner	p. 83 / f. 248v
Dukworth	George		Colcestrian	p. 82 / f. 246v
Duryvall	William		foreigner	p. 84 / f. 249v
Dyng	John		Colcestrian	p. 81 / f. 246r
Edon	William		Colcestrian	p. 81 / f. 246v
Edon	William	(junior)	foreigner	p. 83 / f. 248v
Ekford	Nicholas		foreigner	p. 83 / f. 249r
Elyngham	Thomas		Colcestrian	p. 82 / f. 246v
Elys	John		Colcestrian	p. 81 / f. 246r
Emmys	Robert		foreigner	p. 83 / f. 248v
Erlyng	John		foreigner	p. 83 / f. 248r
Estgate	Richard		foreigner	p. 82 / f. 247v
Everard	John		Colcestrian	p. 81 / f. 246r
Fannyng	John		foreigner	p. 83 / f. 248v
Fen	Clement		Colcestrian	p. 82 / f. 246v
Fenkell	John		foreigner	p. 84 / f. 249v
Fennyng	Thomas		foreigner	p. 83 / f. 248r
Fennyng	Henry		foreigner	p. 83 / f. 248v
Flyngant	William		Colcestrian	p. 82 / f. 246v
Flyngant	John		foreigner	p. 82 / f. 247v
Flyngant	Thomas		foreigner	p. 83 / f. 249r
Foot[5]	John		Colcestrian	p. 81 / f. 246r
Foot	Garard		foreigner	p. 83 / f. 249r
Foster	Andrew		foreigner	p. 82 / f. 247v
Frannceys	William		foreigner	p. 83 / f. 248r
Frannceys	Robert		foreigner	p. 83 / f. 249r
Freget	John	(senior)	Colcestrian	p. 82 / f. 247r
Freget	John	(junior)	Colcestrian	p. 82 / f. 247r
Frenssh	John		Colcestrian	p. 82 / f. 247r
Fuller	Thomas		foreigner	p. 82 / f. 247v

Fullom	John		foreigner	p. 83 / f. 249r
Furneys	John		Colcestrian	p. 82 / f. 247r
Ganday	William		foreigner	p. 83 / f. 249r
Garard	John		foreigner	p. 82 / f. 247v
Gauncele	William		foreigner	p. 82 / f. 248r
George	John		Colccstrian	p. 82 / f. 247r
Geveyn	John		Colcestrian	p. 82 / f. 246v
Gilbert	John		foreigner	p. 82 / f. 247v
Gilder, a	John		foreigner	p. 82 / f. 248r
Giles	Walter		foreigner	p. 83 / f. 249r
Gilford	William		Colcestrian	p. 82 / f. 246v
Gille	John		Colcestrian	p. 82 / f. 246v
Glesene	John		Colcestrian	p. 82 / f. 246v
Goday	William		foreigner	p. 83 / f. 249r
Godston	Robert		foreigner	p. 83 / f. 249r
Gogger	John		foreigner	p. 83 / f. 249r
Good	John	(senior)	foreigner	p. 83 / f. 248r
Gossefeld	William		Colcestrian	p. 82 / f. 247r
Gossefeld	William		foreigner	p. 82 / f. 247v
Gossefeld	William		foreigner	p. 83 / f. 248v
Gossefeld	John		foreigner	p. 83 / f. 249r
Gossefeld	John		foreigner	p. 83 / f. 249r
Grene	John		Colcestrian	p. 81 / f. 246r
Grene	John		foreigner	p. 82 / f. 247v
Grenelef	John		foreigner	p. 83 / f. 248r
Greye	John		foreigner	p. 83 / f. 248v
Hachedy	John		Colcestrian	p. 81 / f. 246r
Hale	John		foreigner	p. 83 / f. 248v
Hamond	William		foreigner	p. 83 / f. 249r
Hamond	John		foreigner	p. 83 / f. 249r
Hampton	John		Colcestrian	p. 82 / f. 246v
Hanteyn [?Hauteyn]	… [?John]	(senior)	foreigner	p. 82 / f. 248r
Hauteyn	John	(junior)	Colcestrian	p. 82 / f. 247r
Helpisby	William		Colcestrian	p. 82 / f. 247r
Hergest	John		Colcestrian	p. 82 / f. 246v
Hermanson	… [Edmund?]	foreigner	p. 83 / f. 249r	
Hermanson	Rumbor		foreigner	p. 83 / f. 249r
Hervy	George		Colcestrian	p. 81 / f. 246r
Hervy	Richard		foreigner	p. 82 / f. 248r
Hervy	John		foreigner	p. 83 / f. 249r
Hethyngham	Thomas		foreigner	p. 83 / f. 248r
Hierde	Robert		foreigner	p. 83 / f. 248v
Hill	William	cook	Colcestrian	p. 82 / f. 247r
Hill	Robert		foreigner	p. 82 / f. 247v
Hobelot	Thomas		foreigner	p. 83 / f. 249r
Hogon	John		foreigner	p. 83 / f. 248r
Holder	John		Colcestrian	p. 82 / f. 246v
Holier	William		Colcestrian	p. 82 / f. 246v
Hook	John		Colcestrian	p. 82 / f. 246v
Horn	John		Colcestrian	p. 82 / f. 246v
Howell	Thomas		foreigner	p. 83 / f. 249r

Howell	John		foreigner	p. 83 / f. 249v
Hynde	Robert		foreigner	p. 82 / f. 247v
Jakes	...		foreigner	p. 82 / f. 248r
James	William		Colcestrian	p. 81 / f. 246v
James	Martin		foreigner	p. 83 / f. 248r
Jamysson	Dederick		Colcestrian	p. 82 / f. 246v
John	Nicholas		foreigner	p. 83 / f. 248v
John	William		foreigner	p. 83 / f. 249r
John	William		foreigner	p. 84 / f. 249v
Johnson	... [?Henry]		foreigner	p. 82 / f. 248r
Johnson	Henry		foreigner	p. 83 / f. 248r
Johnson	Giles		foreigner	p. 83 / f. 248r
Johnson	John		foreigner	p. 83 / f. 248r
Johnson	Garard		foreigner	p. 83 / f. 249r
Joyer	John		Colcestrian	p. 81 / f. 246r
Katrik	Robert		Colcestrian	p. 82 / f. 247r
Kebull	John		foreigner	p. 83 / f. 249v
Kempe	John		Colcestrian	p. 82 / f. 246v
Kendale	George		Colcestrian	p. 82 / f. 247r
Kernor (?Kervor)[6]	William		foreigner	p. 83 / f. 249r
Kersey	Thomas		Colcestrian	p. 81 / f. 246r
Kiriell	Thomas		Colcestrian	p. 82 / f. 246v
Knolles	Edmund		Colcestrian	p. 82 / f. 246v
Kyng	John		Colcestrian	p. 82 / f. 247r
Kyng	William		Colcestrian	p. 82 / f. 247r
Kynggesbury	John		foreigner	p. 83 / f. 248v
Lak	William		foreigner	p. 83 / f. 248v
Lakeman	John		foreigner	p. 83 / f. 248v
Lalleford	Richard		Colcestrian	p. 82 / f. 247r
Lalleford	Thomas		foreigner	p. 83 / f. 248r
Lambard	John	(senior)	Colcestrian	p. 82 / f. 246v
Lambard	John	(junior)	Colcestrian	p. 82 / f. 246v
Langthorn	John		Colcestrian	p. 82 / f. 246v
Langtone	William		Colcestrian	p. 82 / f. 247r
Late	John	(senior)	foreigner	p. 82 / f. 248r
Legge	Robert		foreigner	p. 83 / f. 248v
Lelywhight	Walter		foreigner	p. 82 / f. 247v
Leveson	John		foreigner	p. 83 / f. 249r
Lienge	John		foreigner	p. 83 / f. 249v
Lister	John		Colcestrian	p. 82 / f. 247r
Litewyn	John		Colcestrian	p. 81 / f. 246r
Litewyn[7]	John		foreigner	p. 82 / f. 247v
Litilton	William		Colcestrian	p. 82 / f. 246v
Lolyngton	Robert		foreigner	p. 83 / f. 249v
London	John		Colcestrian	p. 81 / f. 246r
London	William		foreigner	p. 82 / f. 247v
London	Roger		foreigner	p. 83 / f. 248v
Longe	William		foreigner	p. 83 / f. 248r
Loundes/Lonndes[8]	John		Colcestrian	p. 82 / f. 247r
Louthe	Richard		foreigner	p. 82 / f. 247v
Louthe	John		foreigner	p. 82 / f. 247v

Lovell	Thomas		foreigner	p. 82 / f. 247v
Lunte	Henry		foreigner	p. 83 / f. 248v
Lunte	Nicholas		foreigner	p. 83 / f. 249r
Lyard	John		foreigner	p. 83 / f. 249v
Lyon	John		foreigner	p. 83 / f. 248r
Ma...[9]	Robert		Colcestrian	p. 82 / f. 246v
Man	John	carter	foreigner	p. 83 / f. 249r
Man	William	bowyer	foreigner	p. 83 / f. 249v
Mangils	Robert		foreigner	p. 82 / f. 248r
Manser	William		foreigner	p. 83 / f. 248v
Mansfeld	John		Colcestrian	p. 81 / f. 246v
Marchall	Richard		foreigner	p. 83 / f. 248r
Martyn	Roger		Colcestrian	p. 82 / f. 246v
Martyn	John		Colcestrian	p. 82 / f. 246v
Martyn	Edmund		Colcestrian	p. 82 / f. 247r
Martyn	William		foreigner	p. 82 / f. 248r
Martyn	Thomas		foreigner	p. 83 / f. 248r
Martyn	John		foreigner	p. 83 / f. 249v
Mason	William		foreigner	p. 83 / f. 248v
Mawesyn	Nicholas		foreigner	p. 82 / f. 247v
Medewe	William		Colcestrian	p. 82 / f. 247r
Mellor	Thomas		foreigner	p. 83 / f. 248r
Merveyn	John	(senior)	foreigner	p. 83 / f. 248v
Milk	Richard		Colcestrian	p. 81 / f. 246r
Morton	Richard		foreigner	p. 83 / f. 249v
Mot	William		foreigner	p. 82 / f. 247v
Mot	Richard		foreigner	p. 82 / f. 247v
Mud	Adrian		foreigner	p. 82 / f. 248r
Myche	John		Colcestrian	p. 81 / f. 246r
Mynche	Stephen		foreigner	p. 83 / f. 249r
Mynstre	Ambrose		Colcestrian	p. 82 / f. 247r
Naks(?)	John		foreigner	p. 83 / f. 249v
Neve	William		foreigner	p. 83 / f. 248v
Newman	John		Colcestrian	p. 81 / f. 246v
Newman	William		Colcestrian	p. 82 / f. 247r
Newman	Robert		foreigner	p. 82 / f. 247v
Nicollisson	William		foreigner	p. 83 / f. 248v
Noreys	Geoffrey		foreigner	p. 82 / f. 248r
Norman	Adam		foreigner	p. 83 / f. 249v
Norman	Richard		foreigner	p. 83 / f. 249v
Norman	Thomas		foreigner	p. 83 / f. 249v
Norman	William		foreigner	p. 83 / f. 249v
Norton	William		Colcestrian	p. 81 / f. 246r
Nustede	Richard		foreigner	p. 82 / f. 247v
Ody	John		Colcestrian	p. 81 / f. 246r
Ogle	Thomas		Colcestrian	p. 82 / f. 247r
Oker	John		Colcestrian	p. 81 / f. 246r
Olyver	John		foreigner	p. 83 / f. 248r
Oranessen	John		foreigner	p. 83 / f. 249v
Osbern	Henry		foreigner	p. 82 / f. 248r
Osberne	Laurence		foreigner	p. 83 / f. 249v

Oter	John		foreigner	p. 83 / f. 248r
Pach	Robert		Colcestrian	p. 81 / f. 246r
Pach	Richard		foreigner	p. 83 / f. 248v
Pakhe (Patch?)	Richard	(senior)	foreigner	p. 83 / f. 248v
Palmer	Richard		Colcestrian	p. 82 / f. 247r
Park	John		foreigner	p. 83 / f. 249r
Parker	John	mercer	Colcestrian	p. 81 / f. 246r
Parker	William		foreigner	p. 83 / f. 248r
Parker	Robert		foreigner	p. 83 / f. 248r
Parker	Thurstan		foreigner	p. 83 / f. 248r
Parker	Richard	butcher	foreigner	p. 83 / f. 249v
Parys	John		Colcestrian	p. 82 / f. 246v
Parys	John	cook	Colcestrian	p. 82 / f. 246v
Passant	John	(junior)	Colcestrian	p. 82 / f. 247r
Patche	Richard	(junior)	foreigner	p. 83 / f. 248v
Payn	John	(junior)	foreigner	p. 83 / f. 249r
Peak	Robert		foreigner	p. 84 / f. 249v
Pecok	Richard		Colcestrian	p. 81 / f. 246r
Pende	Thomas		foreigner	p. 82 / f. 247v
Pendrell	William		foreigner	p. 83 / f. 249r
Pepard	Henry		foreigner	p. 83 / f. 249r
Perkyn	Robert		Colcestrian	p. 81 / f. 246r
Perpyt	Henry		foreigner	p. 83 / f. 249v
Person	William		Colcestrian	p. 82 / f. 247r
Person	John		foreigner	p. 83 / f. 248v
Peryngton	Robert		Colcestrian	p. 82 / f. 246v
Peter	Henry		foreigner	p. 83 / f. 248r
Peyton	John		foreigner	p. 83 / f. 248v
Philip	Thomas		Colcestrian	p. 82 / f. 247r
Picard	Geoffrey		Colcestrian	p. 82 / f. 246v
Picot	John		foreigner	p. 83 / f. 248r
Piers	John		foreigner	p. 83 / f. 248r
Piers	James		foreigner	p. 83 / f. 248r
Piers	William		foreigner	p. 83 / f. 248v
Pigeys	John		foreigner	p. 84 / f. 249v
Pikerell	John		foreigner	p. 83 / f. 248v
Pilbergh	John		foreigner	p. 83 / f. 249r
Pilgryme	John		foreigner	p. 83 / f. 248v
Pilgryme	Peter		foreigner	p. 83 / f. 248v
Plomer	Richard		Colcestrian	p. 82 / f. 247r
Pollye	William		Colcestrian	p. 82 / f. 246v
Polvele	William		foreigner	p. 83 / f. 248r
Pope	Thomas		Colcestrian	p. 82 / f. 246v
Porter	Robert		Colcestrian	p. 81 / f. 246v
Porter	John		foreigner	p. 83 / f. 249r
Potage	Robert		Colcestrian	p. 82 / f. 247r
Potard	John		Colcestrian	p. 81 / f. 246v
Potard	John	(junior)	Colcestrian	p. 82 / f. 247r
Prentys	William		Colcestrian	p. 82 / f. 247r
Preston	Robert		foreigner	p. 83 / f. 248r
Pudney	Thomas		foreigner	p. 83 / f. 249r

Purser	Peter		Colcestrian	p. 82 / f. 246v
Puttock	Thomas		foreigner	p. 84 / f. 249v
Pynchebek	John		foreigner	p. 82 / f. 247v
Quarmouth, of	John		Colcestrian	p. 82 / f. 247r
Quyntyn	Richard		foreigner	p. 82 / f. 247v
Randele	Richard		foreigner	p. 83 / f. 249v
Randolf	Thomas		foreigner	p. 82 / f. 247v
Rede	John		Colcestrian	p. 82 / f. 246v
Reed	William		foreigner	p. 82 / f. 247v
Rees	John		foreigner	p. 83 / f. 248v
Reve	John		foreigner	p. 83 / f. 249r
Reynham	Thomas		foreigner	p. 83 / f. 248v
Reynold	William		foreigner	p. 83 / f. 248r
Reynold	John		foreigner	p. 83 / f. 248v
Reynold	Robert		foreigner	p. 83 / f. 249r
Reynold	William		foreigner	p. 83 / f. 249r
Reynsford	Henry		Colcestrian	p. 82 / f. 246v
Rippyngale	William		foreigner	p. 83 / f. 248v
Rodehans	…		foreigner	p. 82 / f. 248r
Roger	Richard		Colcestrian	p. 82 / f. 247r
Rokewode	Robert		foreigner	p. 83 / f. 249r
Roos	William		foreigner	p. 83 / f. 249r
Rotelond	John		foreigner	p. 83 / f. 249r
Rous	Thomas		foreigner	p. 82 / f. 247v
Rowgs	John		foreigner	p. 83 / f. 248v
Ruffle	John		foreigner	p. 83 / f. 248r
Russhlyn	John		Colcestrian	p. 82 / f. 247r
Sak(?)	John		foreigner	p. 83 / f. 249r
Sancer	William		Colcestrian	p. 81 / f. 246v
Sayer	Robert		foreigner	p. 82 / f. 247v
Sayer	John		foreigner	p. 83 / f. 249r
Screvener	Robert		foreigner	p. 83 / f. 249v
Sencleer	John		foreigner	p. 83 / f. 248r
Sewhale	John	mercer	foreigner	p. 83 / f. 248v
Sexteyn	John		Colcestrian	p. 81 / f. 246r
Shellesley	Robert		Colcestrian	p. 82 / f. 247r
Shemyng	John		Colcestrian	p. 82 / f. 246v
Sherewyn	Thomas		foreigner	p. 83 / f. 249r
Sherman	Thomas		Colcestrian	p. 82 / f. 246v
Sherman	Robert		foreigner	p. 83 / f. 248v
Shipman	Robert		foreigner	p. 83 / f. 248r
Shipman	John		foreigner	p. 83 / f. 248v
Silvestre	John		foreigner	p. 83 / f. 248v
Skelton	John		Colcestrian	p. 82 / f. 246v
Skirwit	Robert		foreigner	p. 83 / f. 248v
Skymder	…		foreigner	p. 82 / f. 248r
Skynner	John		Colcestrian	p. 82 / f. 246v
Skynner	Thomas		Colcestrian	p. 82 / f. 247r
Smalpece	John		Colcestrian	p. 82 / f. 247r
Smyth	Hugh		Colcestrian	p. 82 / f. 246v
Smyth	John	barber	foreigner	p. 82 / f. 247v

Smyth	John		foreigner	p. 82 / f. 247v
Smyth	Thomas		foreigner	p. 82 / f. 248r
Smyth	John		foreigner	p. 83 / f. 248v
Smyth	John		foreigner	p. 83 / f. 249v
Smyth	Thomas		foreigner	p. 83 / f. 249v
Snellyng	Robert	(senior)	foreigner	p. 83 / f. 248r
Snellyng	John	(junior)	foreigner	p. 83 / f. 248r
Snellyng	John	(senior)	foreigner	p. 83 / f. 248r
Soman	Nuchol(?)		foreigner	p. 83 / f. 248v
Soman	Harry		foreigner	p. 83 / f. 248v
Somersete	William		Colcestrian	p. 82 / f. 247r
Sonday	Thomas		Colcestrian	p. 81 / f. 246r
Sonday	William		foreigner	p. 83 / f. 249v
Sonde	William		Colcestrian	p. 82 / f. 246v
Sonde	John		foreigner	p. 83 / f. 249v
Sparowe	Thomas		Colcestrian	p. 82 / f. 246v
Spery	Edmund		foreigner	p. 83 / f. 248v
Spicer	Stephen		foreigner	p. 82 / f. 248r
Spring	Walter		foreigner	p. 82 / f. 247v
Staldham	Henry		foreigner	p. 83 / f. 248r
Stanford	James		foreigner	p. 83 / f. 248v
Starlyng	Robert		foreigner	p. 83 / f. 249v
Stepill	John		foreigner	p. 83 / f. 249v
Stevens	Thomas		foreigner	p. 83 / f. 249v
Stokeon	Peter		foreigner	p. 82 / f. 247v
Stondon	John		foreigner	p. 82 / f. 247v
Stone	John		Colcestrian	p. 82 / f. 246v
Stone	[?Tho]mas		Colcestrian	p. 82 / f. 247r
Strange	John		Colcestrian	p. 82 / f. 247r
Sutton	John		Colcestrian	p. 81 / f. 246r
Sutton	William		foreigner	p. 82 / f. 247v
Swayn	John		Colcestrian	p. 82 / f. 246v
Swayn	Thomas		foreigner	p. 82 / f. 247v
Swynton	Robert		Colcestrian	p. 82 / f. 246v
Symson	Robert		foreigner	p. 83 / f. 249r
Tashell	John		foreigner	p. 83 / f. 249v
Tasseler	Thomas		foreigner	p. 83 / f. 249r
Tassell	Roger		foreigner	p. 83 / f. 249r
Tedde	Thomas		Colcestrian	p. 82 / f. 246v
Templer	John		foreigner	p. 82 / f. 247v
Teryngton	Henry		foreigner	p. 83 / f. 248v
Teryngton	John		foreigner	p. 83 / f. 248v
Their	Thomas		foreigner	p. 83 / f. 249r
Thirkild	Sampson		foreigner	p. 83 / f. 248r
Thirlby	John		foreigner	p. 83 / f. 249v
Thomson	John		Colcestrian	p. 82 / f. 247r
Thomson	John		foreigner	p. 83 / f. 249v
Thorn	John		foreigner	p. 82 / f. 247v
Thursk	Robert		foreigner	p. 83 / f. 248v
Thurstey(n)	Reginald		foreigner	p. 83 / f. 249v
Thursteyn	John	labourer	foreigner	p. 82 / f. 247v

Thursteyn	Thomas		foreigner	p. 83 / f. 248v
Thursteyn	William		foreigner	p. 83 / f. 248v
Thursteyn	William		foreigner	p. 83 / f. 249r
Thursteyn	Jocardus		foreigner	p. 83 / f. 249r
Thursteyn	Richard	tiler	foreigner	p. 83 / f. 249v
Thusk	John		Colcestrian	p. 81 / f. 246r
Trill	Thomas		Colcestrian	p. 82 / f. 247r
Triplowe	John		Colcestrian	p. 82 / f. 247r
Turnour	Stephen		foreigner	p. 82 / f. 247v
Turnour	John		foreigner	p. 83 / f. 248v
Tyler	John		Colcestrian	p. 82 / f. 246v
Upchar	John		Colcestrian	p. 81 / f. 246v
Upton	John		Colcestrian	p. 82 / f. 246v
Valeys	John		foreigner	p. 83 / f. 249r
Vccr	John		Colcestrian	p. 82 / f. 247r
Veer	Nicholas		foreigner	p. 82 / f. 247v
Veer	Robert		foreigner	p. 83 / f. 248r
Vertue	John		foreigner	p. 83 / f. 249r
Vocat	Nicholas		foreigner	p. 82 / f. 247v
Volantyn	William		foreigner	p. 83 / f. 249r
Vorrant	Edward		foreigner	p. 83 / f. 249v
Vyncent	John		Colcestrian	p. 82 / f. 247r
Vyoll	John		Colcestrian	p. 82 / f. 247r
Waite	John		Colcestrian	p. 81 / f. 246r
Walker	John		foreigner	p. 83 / f. 248r
Waren	John		Colcestrian	p. 82 / f. 247r
Wary[n?]	Roger		Colcestrian	p. 82 / f. 247r
Waryn	Thomas		foreigner	p. 82 / f. 247v
Wasse	William		foreigner	p. 83 / f. 249r
Wastelyn	Thomas		Colcestrian	p. 82 / f. 246v
Water	Ailewin		foreigner	p. 82 / f. 248r
Watier	James		foreigner	p. 82 / f. 247v
Webbe	Thomas		foreigner	p. 82 / f. 247v
Webbe	John		foreigner	p. 83 / f. 249r
Webbe	John		foreigner	p. 84 / f. 249v
Weder	Peter		Colcestrian	p. 82 / f. 247r
Welsmyth	John		Colcestrian	p. 82 / f. 247r
Wer	William		Colcestrian	p. 82 / f. 247r
Wesden	Thomas		foreigner	p. 83 / f. 248v
West	Roger		foreigner	p. 83 / f. 248v
West	John		foreigner	p. 83 / f. 249v
Whitby	Robert		Colcestrian	p. 82 / f. 247r
Whitehed	John		Colcestrian	p. 82 / f. 247r
Wigen	Richard		foreigner	p. 83 / f. 248v
Wilde	John		foreigner	p. 82 / f. 247v
Wilkyns	Roger		Colcestrian	p. 82 / f. 246v
Willis	Thomas		Colcestrian	p. 82 / f. 247r
Willymot	William		foreigner	p. 83 / f. 248v
Willymot	Thomas		foreigner	p. 83 / f. 248v
Wilton	John		Colcestrian	p. 82 / f. 247r
Wilton	Walter		foreigner	p. 83 / f. 248r

Wode	John	foreigner	p. 83 / f. 248v
Wodeles	William	foreigner	p. 82 / f. 247v
Wogayn	Austyn	foreigner	p. 84 / f. 249v
Worthy	John	Colcestrian	p. 82 / f. 246v
Wortier	John	Colcestrian	p. 81 / f. 246r
Wrighte	Gilbert	foreigner	p. 82 / f. 247v
Wrighte	Robert	foreigner	p. 82 / f. 247v
Wymond	Richard	Colcestrian	p. 82 / f. 247r
Yates	Thomas	foreigner	p. 83 / f. 248v
Yerdes	John	foreigner	p. 83 / f. 248v
Yon	John	foreigner	p. 84 / f. 249v
Yonge	Thomas	foreigner	p. 83 / f. 248v
Yvy	Edmund	foreigner	p. 83 / f. 248v

Appendix 3
Mediaeval Colchester Street Names

Not all the town centre streets are mentioned in the surviving records. Those whose names are recorded are listed below with their modern equivalents. Castle Road, Roman Road, Sir Isaac's Walk and Southway did not exist in the Middle Ages.

Mediaeval name	Modern name
Balkerne Lane	Balkerne Hill
Bere Lane (Beris Lane)	Vineyard Street
Botolph Street	St Botolph's Street
Catte Lane	Lion Walk
Corn Hill	western end of High Street
Croucherche Lane	Crouch Street
Culver Lane	Culver Street East and Culver Street West
East Stockwell Street	East Stockwell Street
East Street	East Hill and modern East Street
Elde Lane	Eld Lane
Elyn Lane	St Helen's Lane
Frere Street	eastern end of High Street from the East Gate to St Nicholas Street
Gutter Street (? 18th-century evidence)	St John's Street
Hed Street	Headgate Street
Helle Lane	? Bank Passage
Hog Lane	Mersey Road / Magdalen Street

Stones from St John's Abbey reused to form the pier of a gateway into the Colchester Garrison, in the abbey precinct wall, Flagstaff Road.

Mediaeval name	Modern name
Holmere Lane	Butt Road
Lodders Lane	Abbeygate Street
Lyard Lane	Butt Road
Magdaleyne Lane	Magdalen Street
Maidenburgh Street	Maidenburgh Street north of William's Walk
Maldon Lane	Maldon Road
More Elm Lane	a lane leading south or east from More (Priory) Street, perhaps the modern private road leading to J. Watts
More Street	Priory Street
North Street	North Hill
South Street	Queen Street
Trinity Lane	Trinity Street
West Stockwell Street	West Stockwell Street
Wyre Street	Long and Short Wyre Streets

Appendix 4
Dating

Three points need to be made about the dates given in this book, since these might appear confusing to readers not accustomed to the problems of the mediaeval dating systems.

1. In mediaeval England the calendar year did not begin on 1 January but on Lady Day (25 March). For this reason dates between 1 January and 24 March, which in modern terms would fall at the **start** of the year, actually fell at the **end** of the preceding year in mediaeval terms. It is conventional for historians to give two year dates in such cases, for example 16 February 1461/2. This means 16 February 1462 by modern dating – but mediaeval writers would have called it 16 February 1461.

2. In mediaeval Colchester the civic year of office for the bailiffs and other officials ran from Michaelmas Day (29 September) and thus overlapped two calendar years. For this reason reference to Colchester records usually have year dates in the form 1461–62.

3. Mediaeval writers often dated events by the feasts of the church and by the year of the reigning monarch: thus, for example 'Candlemas, 5 Edward IV' would refer to the feast of Candlemas [2 February] in the fifth year of Edward IV's reign. Such dates have been retained in this book, but for the convenience of readers they have also been converted into standard calendar dates enclosed in square brackets.

Notes

1. Soc. Ant., MS 77, ff. 4v, 5r; *HHB*, part 2, p. 288.

2. There may be some discrepancies. The list includes six persons named as 'senior' for whom there is no corresponding 'junior', and six persons named as 'junior' for whom there is no corresponding 'senior'. This suggests that some of the men of Colchester may have been absent (unless they were resident elsewhere).

3. The list is taken mainly from W. G. Benham, ed., *The Red Paper Book of Colchester*, pp. 81–84, but some errors and gaps in Benham's transcription have been tentatively corrected from other sources.

4. Benham offers 'Bovere' as a possible alternative reading but no such surname is elsewhere attested in Colchester at this period.

5   Benham offers 'Feet' as a possible alternative reading but no such surname is elsewhere recorded in Colchester at this period.

6   Neither surname is elsewhere attested in Colchester at this period.

7. Benham's published transcript gives 'Eitwyn'.

8. Perhaps this refers to John Loundy.

9. Robert **Martyn** and Robert **Marynere** are both attested in Colchester at about this period.

BIBLIOGRAPHY

A Guide to Many of Colchester's Churches, Colchester 2001.

Ashdown-Hill, J. *Yesterday my Lord of Gloucester came to Colchester*, Essex *Archaeology and History*, vol. 36 (2005), pp.212–17.

———— 'The client network, connections and patronage of Sir John, Lord Howard, first Duke of Norfolk, in north east Essex and south Suffolk', unpublished PhD thesis, University of Essex, 2008.

Baldwin, D. *The Lost Prince*, Stroud, 2007.

Benfield, S. 'The lost Church of the Crossed Friars', *The Colchester Archaeologist*, no.20 (2007), pp.19–23.

Benham, W.G. ed., *The Red Paper Book of Colchester*, Colchester, 1902.

———— *The Oath Book or Red Parchment Book of Colchester*, Colchester, 1907.

Britnell, R.H. *Colchester in the Fifteenth Century – a Portrait*, http://www.dur.ac.uk/r.h.britnell/Portrait%203htm (consulted June 2008).

Bruton, E. *The History of Clocks and Watches*, London, 1979.

Burgess, C. 'A service for the dead: the form and function of the anniversary in late mediaeval Bristol', in Blake, S.T. and Saville, A. eds., *Transactions of the Bristol and Gloucestershire Archaeological Society for 1987*, vol. 105, pp.183–211.

Cockayne, G.E. *The Complete Peerage*, London, 1910–59.

Cockerill, C. and Woodward, D. *Colchester Churches a brief history and description*, Colchester, 1973.

Crawford, A. ed., *The Household Books of John Howard, Duke of Norfolk, 1462–1471, 1481–1483*, Stroud, 1992.

Denney, P. *The Changing Face of Colchester*, Derby, 2002.

Dugdale, W. (Caley, J., Ellis, H. & Bandinel, B. eds), *Monasticon Anglicanum*, vol. 4b, London, 1846.

Galloway, J.A. *Colchester and its region, 1310–1560. Wealth, Industry and Rural-Urban mobility in a Mediaeval Society*, unpublished PhD thesis, University of Edinburgh, 1986.

Gamble, D.J. *St Giles's Church*, Colchester, 1998.

Karras, R.M. *Common Women*, Oxford, 1996.

Kirk R.E.G. ed., *Feet of Fines for Essex, 1182–1272*, Essex Archaeological Society 1899–1910, vol. 1.

Letters & Papers Foreign & Domestic: Henry VIII, 1509–13, London, 1862–1932.

McCall, A. *The Mediaeval Underworld*, London, 1979.

Mason, B. *Clock and Watchmaking in Colchester, England*, London, 1969.

Moore, S.A. ed., *Cartularium Monasterii Sancti Iohannis Bapiste de Colcestria*, 2 vols. London, 1897.

Otis, L.L. *Prostitution in Mediaeval Society*, Chicago and London, 1985.

Peers C.R. *St Botolph's Priory, Colchester*, HMSO, 1917.

Prockter, A. and Taylor, R. *The A to Z of Elizabethan London*, London, 1979.

RCHM, vol. 2 (*South West Essex*), 1921; vol. 3 (*North East Essex*), 1922.

Reeves, C. *Pleasures and Pastimes in Mediaeval England*, Stroud, 1997.

Ridgard, J. ed., *Mediaeval Framlingham*, Suffolk Record Society, vol. 27, Woodbridge, 1985.

Rimmer, A. *Ancient Stone Crosses of England*, London, 1875 (also reprinted 1973).

Robertson, D.W. *Chaucer's London*, New York, 1968.

Round, J.H. *Register of the Scholars admitted to the Colchester School 1637–1740*, Colchester, 1897.

The Colchester Archaeologist, no. 20 (2007).

Thornton, C. *Bourne Mill Colchester – Historical Report*, unpublished, December 2007 (copies in the Colchester Public Library – Local Studies section and at the Essex Record Office).

Victoria County History of Essex, volumes 2 and 9.

Website of the Augustinian Canons Regular (consulted March 2008).

Website of the English Benedictine Congregation (consulted March 2008).

Weever, J. *Ancient Funeral Monuments of Great Britain*, London, 1631 (also reprinted London 1767 and Amsterdam 1979).

INDEX